T0028675

EVERYMAN,
I WILL GO WITH THEE
AND BE THY GUIDE,
IN THY MOST NEED
TO GO BY THY SIDE

EVERYMAN'S LIBRARY
POCKET POETS

MUSIC'S SPELL

POEMS ABOUT MUSIC AND MUSICIANS

••••••••••••••••••

EDITED
BY EMILY FRAGOS

EVERYMAN'S LIBRARY
POCKET POETS

Alfred A. Knopf New York London Toronto

THIS IS A BORZOI BOOK

PUBLISHED BY ALFRED A. KNOPF

This selection by Emily Fragos first published in
Everyman's Library, 2009
Copyright © 2009 by Everyman's Library

Sixth printing (US)

A list of acknowledgments to copyright owners appears at the back
of this volume.

www.randomhouse.com/everymans
www.everymanslibrary.co.uk

ISBN 978-0-307-27092-4 (US)
978-1-84159-783-6 (UK)

A CIP catalogue record for this book is available from the British Library

Library of Congress Cataloging-in-Publication Data
Music's spell: poems about music and musicians / edited by Emily Fragos.
p.   cm.—(Everyman's Library pocket poets)
Includes bibliographical references and index.
ISBN 978-0-307-27092-4 (alk. paper)
1. Music—Poetry. 2. Fragos, Emily.
PN6110.M7M86   2009   2008042855
808.81'93578—dc22

Typography by Peter B. Willberg

Typeset in the UK by AccComputing, North Barrow, Somerset

Printed and bound in Germany by GGP Media GmbH, Pössneck

CONTENTS

POP, ROCK

JAZZ, BLUES

COMPOSERS

THE OPUS

10

11

MUSIC AT THE CLOSE

FOREWORD

Hearts swell at the sound of a ravishing voice, a melancholy guitar, an oboe's floating cry. Jazz riffs lead us through a maze of moods we recognize as our own perhaps for the first time. Shakespeare's galloping horses stop in their tracks at the hearing of a captivating melody. Rock concerts with their waves and walls of sound release from pent-up bodies the deepest energies. How to explain the transformative, expressive power of music in our lives – this music we create with our own breath and our own hands?

Though music is a language without words – the "language where all language ends," as Rilke has it – the impulse to explain it in words is an old and abiding one. The ancient Greeks believed that the planets produced "music of the spheres," profoundly exquisite harmonies, as they revolved in their orbits. Thus, although we cannot hear these celestial sounds, our souls, attuned to harmony from birth, respond to music created on Earth. We are surrounded, inundated even, by music: "There's music in all things, if men had ears:/Their earth is but an echo of the spheres," wrote Lord Byron.

Poets in particular have been drawn to try to translate music's spell into verbal form, perhaps because theirs is also an art in which the expressive qualities of sound and rhythm and unspoken resonances play a role.

15

This much is certain: music is all important to the human race. It has the power and the charm to move, disturb, sadden, gladden, bring consolation, celebration, salvation. We remember the stages of our lives by the music we heard, sang, danced to. Children's songs we pass on from generation to generation as soothing lullabies. We work and play and love and pray to music.

"Without music," Frederick Nietzsche said, "life would be a mistake." It would be a world without harmony, without singing and dancing – and without poetry, that legacy of the first poet-musician, Orpheus, who with his lyre, so goes the myth, first stirred the soul and bestowed upon the struggling world the sweet power of music.

Emily Fragos

THE POWER
OF MUSIC

Such sweet compulsion doth in music lie.
JOHN MILTON

From THE TEMPEST

Be not afeard: the isle is full of noises,
Sounds and sweet airs, that give delight, and hurt not.
Sometimes a thousand twangling instruments
Will hum about mine ears; and sometimes voices,
That, if I then had wak'd after long sleep,
Will make me sleep again: and then, in dreaming,
The clouds methought would open and show riches
Ready to drop upon me; that, when I wak'd
I cried to dream again.

From THE MOURNING BRIDE

Music has charms to soothe a savage breast,
   To soften rocks, or bend a knotted oak.
      I've read that things inanimate have moved,
         And, as with living souls, have been inform'd,
            By magic numbers and persuasive sound.

TO MUSIC

Music: breathing of statues. Perhaps:
silence of paintings. You language where all language
ends. You time
standing vertically on the motion of mortal hearts.

Feelings for whom? O you the transformation
of feelings into what? – into audible landscape.
You stranger: music. You heart-space
grown out of us. The deepest space *in* us,
which, rising above us, forces its way out, –
holy departure:
when the innermost point in us stands
outside, as the most practiced distance, as the other
side of the air:
pure,
boundless,
no longer habitable.

"THAT MUSIC ALWAYS ROUND ME"

That music always round me, unceasing, unbeginning,
     yet long untaught I did not hear,
But now the chorus I hear and am elated,
A tenor, strong, ascending with power and health,
     with glad notes of daybreak I hear,
A soprano at intervals sailing buoyantly over the tops
     of immense waves,
A transparent bass shuddering lusciously under and
     through the universe,
The triumphant tutti, the funeral wailings with sweet
     flutes and violins, all these I fill myself with,
I hear not the volumes of sound merely, I am moved
     by the exquisite meanings,
I listen to the different voices winding in and out,
     striving, contending with fiery vehemence to
     excel each other in emotion;
I do not think the performers know themselves –
     but now I think I begin to know them.

TWO FRAGMENTS

MUSIC AND SWEET POETRY

How sweet it is to sit and read the tales
　Of mighty poets and to hear the while
Sweet music, which when the attention fails
　Fills the dim pause –

TO MUSIC

Silver key of the fountain of tears
　Where the spirit drinks till the brain is wild;
Softest grave of a thousand fears,
　Where their mother, Care, like a drowsy child,
　　Is laid asleep in flowers.

From A SONG FOR ST CECILIA'S DAY
November 22, 1687

From Harmony, from heav'nly Harmony
    This universal Frame began;
    When Nature underneath a heap
    Of jarring Atomes lay,
    And cou'd not heave her Head,
The tuneful Voice was heard from high,
    Arise, ye more than dead.
Then cold and hot and moist and dry,
    In order to their Stations leap,
    And MUSICK'S pow'r obey.
From Harmony, from heavenly Harmony
    This universal Frame began:
    From Harmony to Harmony
Through all the Compass of the Notes it ran,
The Diapason closing full in Man.

What Passion cannot MUSICK raise and quell?
    When *Jubal* struck the corded Shell,
    His listening Brethren stood around,
    And, wond'ring, on their Faces fell
    To worship that Celestial Sound:
Less than a God they thought there could not dwell
    Within the hollow of that Shell,
    That spoke so sweetly, and so well.
What Passion cannot MUSICK raise and quell?

A CRAZED GIRL

That crazed girl improvising her music,
Her poetry, dancing upon the shore,
Her soul in division from itself
Climbing, falling she knew not where,
Hiding amid the cargo of a steamship,
Her knee-cap broken, that girl I declare
A beautiful lofty thing, or a thing
Heroically lost, heroically found.

No matter what disaster occurred
She stood in desperate music wound,
Wound, wound, and she made in her triumph
Where the bales and the baskets lay
No common intelligible sound
But sang, "O sea-starved, hungry sea."

MUSIC

When music sounds, gone is the earth I know,
And all her lovely things even lovelier grow;
Her flowers in vision flame, her forest trees
Lift burdened branches, stilled with ecstasies.

When music sounds, out of the water rise
Naiads whose beauty dims my waking eyes,
Rapt in strange dreams burns each enchanted face,
With solemn echoing stirs their dwelling-place.

When music sounds, all that I was I am
Ere to this haunt of brooding dust I came;
And from Time's woods break into distant song
The swift-winged hours, as I hasten along.

MUSIC

The neighbour sits in his window and plays the flute.
From my bed I can hear him,
And the round notes flutter and tap about the room,
And hit against each other,
Blurring to unexpected chords.
It is very beautiful,
With the little flute-notes all about me,
In the darkness.

In the daytime,
The neighbour eats bread and onions with one hand
And copies music with the other.
He is fat and has a bald head,
So I do not look at him,
But run quickly past his window.
There is always the sky to look at,
Or the water in the well!

But when night comes and he plays his flute,
I think of him as a young man,
With gold seals hanging from his watch,
And a blue coat with silver buttons.
As I lie in my bed
The flute-notes push against my ears and lips,
And I go to sleep, dreaming.

AMY LOWELL   27

TO MUSIC, TO BECALM
HIS FEVER

Charm me asleep, and melt me so
　　With thy delicious numbers
That, being ravished, hence I go
　　Away in easy slumbers.
　　　Ease my sick head,
　　　And make my bed,
Thou power that canst sever
　　　Me from this ill,
　　　And quickly still,
　　　Thou though not kill
　　　　My fever.

　Thou sweetly canst convert the same
　　From a consuming fire
Into a gentle-licking flame,
　　And make it thus expire.
　　　Then make me weep
　　　My pains asleep,
And give me such reposes
　　　That I, poor I,
　　　May think thereby
　　　I live and die
　　　　'Mongst roses.

Fall on me like a silent dew,
  Or like those maiden showers
Which, by the peep of day, do strew
  A baptism o'er the flowers.
      Melt, melt my pains
      With thy soft strains,
That, having ease me given,
      With full delight
      I leave this light,
      And take my flight
        For heaven.

From THE RIME OF THE ANCIENT MARINER

For when it dawn'd – they dropp'd their arms,
And cluster'd round the mast;
Sweet sounds rose slowly through their mouths,
And from their bodies pass'd.

Around, around, flew each sweet sound,
Then darted to the Sun;
Slowly the sounds came back again,
Now mix'd, now one by one.

Sometimes a-dropping from the sky
I heard the skylark sing;
Sometimes all little birds that are,
How they seem'd to fill the sea and air
With their sweet jargoning!

And now 'twas like all instruments,
Now like a lonely flute;
And now it is an angel's song,
That makes the Heavens be mute.

SONNET

I am in need of music that would flow
Over my fretful, feeling finger-tips,
Over my bitter-tainted, trembling lips,
With melody, deep, clear, and liquid-slow.
Oh, for the healing swaying, old and low,
Of some song sung to rest the tired dead,
A song to fall like water on my head,
And over quivering limbs, dream flushed to glow!

There is a magic made by melody:
A spell of rest, and quiet breath, and cool
Heart, that sinks through fading colors deep
To the subaqueous stillness of the sea,
And floats forever in a moon-green pool,
Held in the arms of rhythm and of sleep.

From AT A SOLEMN MUSICK

Blest pair of Sirens, pledges of Heaven's joy,
Sphere-born harmonious Sisters, Voice and Vers,
Wed your divine sounds, and mixt power employ
Dead things with inbreath'd sense able to pierce,
And to our high-rais'd phantasie present,
That undisturbèd Song of pure concent,
Ay sung before the sapphire-colour'd throne
To Him that sits theron,
With Saintly shout, and solemn Jubily,
Where the bright Seraphim in burning row
Their loud up-lifted Angel trumpets blow,
And the Cherubick host in thousand quires
Touch their immortal Harps of golden wires,
With those just Spirits that wear victorious Palms,
Hymns devout and holy Psalms,
Singing everlastingly;
That we on Earth with undiscording voice
May rightly answer that melodious noise....

TO MUSICK

Musick, thou *Queen of Heaven*, Care-charming-spel,
    That strik'st a stilnesse into hell:
Thou that tam'st *Tygers*, and fierce storms (that rise)
    With thy soule-melting Lullabies:
Fall down, down, down, from those thy chiming spheres,
To charme our soules, as thou enchant'st our eares.

A SONG OF JOYS

O to make the most jubilant song!
Full of music – full of manhood, womanhood, infancy!
Full of common employments – full of grain and trees.

O for the voices of animals – O for the swiftness and
    balance of fishes!
O for the dropping of raindrops in a song!
O for the sunshine and motion of waves in a song!

O the joy of my spirit – it is uncaged – it darts like
    lightning!
It is not enough to have this globe or a certain time,
I will have thousands of globes and all time.

From DEJECTION: AN ODE

O pure of heart! thou need'st not ask of me
What this strong music in the soul may be!
What, and wherein it doth exist,
This light, this glory, this fair luminous mist,
This beautiful and beauty-making power.
   Joy, virtuous Lady! Joy that ne'er was given,
Save to the pure, and in their purest hour,
Life, and Life's effluence, cloud at once and shower,
Joy, Lady! is the spirit and the power,
Which wedding Nature to us gives in dower
   A new Earth and new Heaven,
Undreamt of by the sensual and the proud –
Joy is the sweet voice, Joy the luminous cloud –
     We in ourselves rejoice!
And thence flows all that charms or ear or sight,
   All melodies the echoes of that voice,
All colours a suffusion from that light.

"SLOW, SLOW, FRESH FOUNT"

Slow, slow, fresh fount, keep time with my salt tears;
Yet, slower, yet; O faintly, gentle springs:
List to the heavy part the music bears,
Woe weeps out her division, when she sings.
    Droop herbs, and flowers,
    Fall grief in showers,
    Our beauties are not ours:
       O, I could still,
Like melting snow upon some craggy hill,
    Drop, drop, drop, drop,
Since nature's pride is, now, a withered daffodil.

IN MUSIC

Wailing of a flute, a little drum.
A small wedding cortege accompanies a couple
Going past clay houses on the street of a village.
In the dress of the bride much white satin.
How many pennies put away to sew it, once in a
    lifetime.
The dress of the groom black, festively stiff.
The flute tells something to the hills, parched, the
    color of deer.
Hens scratch in dry mounds of manure.

I have not seen it, I summoned it listening to music.
The instruments play for themselves, in their own
    eternity.
Lips glow, agile fingers work, so short a time.
Soon afterwards the pageant sinks into the earth.
But the sound endures, autonomous, triumphant,
For ever visited by, each time returning,
The warm touch of cheeks, interiors of houses,
And particular human lives
Of which the chronicles make no mention.

CHURCH-MUSICK

Sweetest of sweets, I thank you: when displeasure
    Did through my bodie wound my minde,
You took me thence, and in your house of pleasure
    A daintie lodging me assign'd.

Now I in you without a bodie move
    Rising and falling with your wings:
We both together sweetly live and love,
    Yet say sometimes, *God help poore Kings.*

Comfort, I'le die; for if you poste from me,
    Sure I shall do so, and much more:
But if I travell in your companie,
    You know the way to heavens doore.

THE MORNING WATCH

O joys! Infinite sweetness! With what flowers
And shoots of glory my soul breaks and buds!
        All the long hours
        Of night and rest,
        Through the still shrouds
        Of sleep and clouds
      This dew fell on my breast.
        Oh how it bloods
And spirits all my earth! Hark – in what rings
And hymning circulations the quick world
        Awakes and sings!
        The rising winds,
        And falling springs,
        Birds, beasts – all things –
      Adore him in their kinds.
        Thus all is hurled
In sacred hymns and order, the great chime
And symphony of nature. Prayer is
        The world in tune,
        A spirit voice,
        And vocal joys
      Whose echo is heaven's bliss.
        Oh, let me climb
When I lie down! The pious soul by night
Is like a clouded star whose beams – though said

                    To shed their light
                    Under some cloud –
                    Yet are above,
                    And shine, and move
                Beyond that misty shroud.
                    So in my bed
(That curtained grave), though sleep – like ashes – hide
My lamp and life, both shall in thee abide.

PERPLEXED MUSIC
Affectionately inscribed to E. J.

Experience, like a pale musician, holds
A dulcimer of patience in his hand,
Whence harmonies, we cannot understand,
Of God's will in his worlds, the strain unfolds
In sad-perplexèd minors: deathly colds
Fall on us while we hear, and countermand
Our sanguine heart back from the fancyland
With nightingales in visionary wolds.
We murmur "Where is any certain tune
Or measured music in such notes as these?"
But angels, leaning from the golden seat,
Are not so minded; their fine ear hath won
The issue of completed cadences,
And, smiling down the stars, they whisper – SWEET.

From MICROCOSMUS

The heavens first in tune I'll set,
And from their music soon beget
A charm of power to make light fire
Skip to his sphere and earth retire
To her parched den. The subtle air
I'll calm from mists and make it fair,
And water with her curl'd waves sweep
The bounded channels of the deep,
That order may succeed, and things
Grow perfect from their lasting springs.
More light, ye spheres, in concord sound,
And with your music fill this round!

From ODE ON ST CECILIA'S DAY

Music the fiercest grief can charm,
  And fate's severest rage disarm. Music can soften
      pain to ease,
    And make despair and madness please;
      Our joys below it can improve,
        And antedate the bliss above.

From THE ODYSSEY

So sang the bard illustrious; then his robe
Of purple dye with both hands o'er his head
Ulysses drew, behind its ample folds
Veiling his face, through fear to be observed
By the Phaeacians weeping at the song;
And ever as the bard harmonious ceased,
He wiped his tears, and, drawing from his brows
The mantle, pour'd libation to the Gods.
But when the Chiefs (for they delighted heard
Those sounds) solicited again the bard,
And he renew'd the strain, then cov'ring close
His count'nance, as before, Ulysses wept.

44   HOMER
     TRANS. WILLIAM COWPER

"THE FASCINATING CHILL
THAT MUSIC LEAVES"

The fascinating chill that music leaves
Is Earth's corroboration
Of Ecstasy's impediment –
'Tis Rapture's germination
In timid and tumultuous soil
A fine – estranging creature –
To something upper wooing us
But not to our Creator –

From THE LOTUS-EATERS

There is sweet music here that softer falls
Than petals from blown roses on the grass,
Or night-dews on still waters between walls
Of shadowy granite, in a gleaming pass;
Music that gentlier on the spirit lies,
Than tired eyelids upon tired eyes;
Music that brings sweet sleep down from the
    blissful skies.
Here are cool mosses deep,
And thro' the moss the ivies creep,
And in the stream the long-leaved flowers weep,
And from the craggy ledge the poppy hangs in sleep.

Why are we weigh'd upon with heaviness,
And utterly consumed with sharp distress,
While all things else have rest from weariness?
All things have rest: why should we toil alone,
We only toil, who are the first of things,
And make perpetual moan,
Still from one sorrow to another thrown;
Nor ever fold our wings,
And cease from wanderings,
Nor steep our brows in slumber's holy balm;
Nor harken what the inner spirit sings,
"There is no joy but calm!" –
Why should we only toil, the roof and crown of things?

SONNET: INSIDE OF KING'S COLLEGE CHAPEL, CAMBRIDGE

What awful perspective! While from our sight
With gradual stealth the lateral windows hide
The portraitures, their stone-work glimmers, dyed
In the soft chequerings of a sleepy light.
Martyr, or king, or sainted eremite,
Whoe'er ye be, that thus, yourselves unseen,
Imbue your prison bars with solemn sheen.
Shine on, until ye fade with coming night!
But from the arms of silence – list! oh list!
The music bursteth into second life;
The notes luxuriate, every stone is kissed
By sound, or ghost of sound, in mazy strife;
Heart-thrilling strains, that cast, before the eye
Of the devout, a veil of ecstasy!

SOFT MUSIC

The mellow touch of music most doth wound
The soul, when it doth rather sigh, than sound.

"PIPING DOWN THE VALLEYS WILD"

Piping down the valleys wild,
Piping songs of pleasant glee,
On a cloud I saw a child,
And he laughing said to me:

"Pipe a song about a Lamb!"
So I piped with merry cheer.
"Piper, pipe that song again;"
So I piped: he wept to hear.

"Drop thy pipe, thy happy pipe;
Sing thy songs of happy cheer."
So I sang the same again,
While he wept with joy to hear.

"Piper, sit thee down and write
In a book, that all may read."
So he vanish'd from my sight,
And I pluck'd a hollow reed,

And I made a rural pen,
And I stain'd the water clear,
And I wrote my happy songs
Every child may joy to hear.

WILLIAM BLAKE   49

From DON JUAN

There's music in the sighing of a reed;
   There's music in the gushing of a rill;
      There's music in all things, if men had ears:
      Their earth is but an echo of the spheres.

WHERE EVERYTHING IS MUSIC

Don't worry about saving these songs!
And if one of our instruments breaks,
it doesn't matter.

We have fallen into the place
where everything is music.

The strumming and the flute notes
rise into the atmosphere,
and even if the whole world's harp
should burn up, there will still be
hidden instruments playing.

So the candle flickers and goes out.
We have a piece of flint, and a spark.

This singing art is sea foam.
The graceful movements come from a pearl
somewhere on the ocean floor.

Poems reach up like spindrift and the edge
of driftwood along the beach, wanting!

They derive
from a slow and powerful root
that we can't see.

Stop the words now.
Open the window in the centre of your chest,
and let the spirits fly in and out.

JALALUDDIN RUMI   51
TRANS. COLEMAN BARKS AND JOHN MOYNE

From THE MERCHANT OF VENICE

JESSICA:
I am never merry when I hear sweet music.

LORENZO:
The reason is, your spirits are attentive.
For do but note a wild and wanton herd,
Or race of youthful and unhandled colts,
Fetching mad bounds, bellowing and neighing loud,
Which is the hot condition of their blood;
If they but hear perchance a trumpet sound,
Or any air of music touch their ears,
You shall perceive them make a mutual stand,
Their savage eyes turned to a modest gaze
By the sweet power of music. Therefore the poet
Did feign that Orpheus drew trees, stones, and floods;
Since naught so stockish, hard and full of rage,
But music for the time doth change his nature.
That man that hath no music in himself,
Nor is not moved with concord of sweet sounds,
Is fit for treasons, stratagems, and spoils;
The motions of his spirit are dull as night,
And his affections dark as Erebus.
Let no such man be trusted. Mark the music.

MUSIC AND LOVE

Give me some music; music, moody food
Of us that trade in love.

WILLIAM SHAKESPEARE

JUKE BOX LOVE SONG

I could take the Harlem night
And wrap around you,
Take the neon lights and make a crown,
Take the Lenox Avenue buses,
Taxis, subways,
And for your love song tone their rumble down.
Take Harlem's heartbeat,
Make a drumbeat,
Put it on a record, let it whirl,
And while we listen to it play,
Dance with you till day –
Dance with you, my sweet brown Harlem girl.

TO —

Music, when soft voices die,
Vibrates in the memory –
Odours, when sweet violets sicken,
Live within the sense they quicken.

Rose leaves, when the rose is dead,
Are heaped for the beloved's bed;
And so thy thoughts, when thou art gone,
Love itself shall slumber on.

From TWELFTH NIGHT

If music be the food of love, play on!
Give me excess of it, that, surfeiting,
The appetite may sicken, and so die.
That strain again! It had a dying fall.
O, it came o'er my ear like the sweet sound
That breathes upon a bank of violets,
Stealing and giving odour. Enough! no more!
'Tis not so sweet now as it was before.

WILLIAM SHAKESPEARE

"FOLLOW YOUR SAINT, FOLLOW WITH ACCENTS SWEET"

Follow your saint, follow with accents sweet;
Haste you, sad notes, fall at her flying feet.
There, wrapp'd in cloud of sorrow, pity move,
And tell the ravisher of my soul I perish for her love:
But if she scorns my never-ceasing pain,
Then burst with sighing in her sight and ne'er
     return again.

All that I sung still to her praise did tend,
Still she was first; still she my songs did end;
Yet she my love and music both doth fly,
The music that her echo is and beauty's sympathy.
Then let my notes pursue her scornful flight:
It shall suffice that they were breath'd and died for
     her delight.

AN OLD MEMORY

How sweet the music sounded
That summer long ago,
When you were by my side, love,
To list its gentle flow.

I saw your eyes ashining,
I felt your rippling hair,
I kissed your pearly cheek, love,
And had no thought of care.

And gay or sad the music,
With subtle charm replete;
I found in after years, love,
'Twas you that made it sweet.

For standing where we heard it,
I hear again the strain;
It wakes my heart, but thrills it
With sad, mysterious pain.

It pulses not so joyous
As when you stood with me,
And hand in hand we listened
To that low melody.

Oh, could the years turn back, love!
Oh, could events be changed
To what they were that time, love,
Before we were estranged;

Wert thou once more a maiden
Whose smile was gold to me;
Were I once more the lover
Whose word was life to thee.

O God! could all be altered,
The pain, the grief, the strife,
And wert thou as thou shouldst be,
My true and loyal wife!

But all my tears are idle,
And all my wishes vain.
What once you were to me, love,
You may not be again.

For I, alas! like others,
Have missed my dearest aim.
I asked for love. Oh, mockery!
Fate comes to me with fame!

C MAJOR

When he came down to the street after the
      rendezvous
the air was swirling with snow.
Winter had come
while they lay together.
The night shone white.
He walked quickly with joy.
The whole town was downhill.
The smiles passing by –
everyone was smiling behind turned-up collars.
It was free!
And all the question marks began singing of
      God's being.
So he thought.

A music broke out
and walked in the swirling snow
with long steps.
Everything on the way towards the note C.
A trembling compass directed at C.
One hour higher than the torments.
It was easy!
Behind turned-up collars everyone was smiling.

TOMAS TRANSTRÖMER   61
TRANS. ROBIN FULTON

"YOUR HAND WAS TRYING THE KEYBOARD"

Your hand was trying the keyboard,
your eyes were following the impossible
signs on the sheet: and every chord
was breaking, like a voice in grief.

I noticed everything nearby turn tender,
seeing you helpless stalled unsure
of the language that was most your own:
beyond the half-shut windows the bright sea
    hummed it.

In the blue square butterflies
danced fleetingly: a branch shook in the sun.
Not one thing near us found its words
and your sweet ignorance was mine, was *ours*.

MUSIC I HEARD

Music I heard with you was more than music,
And bread I broke with you was more than bread;
Now that I am without you, all is desolate;
All that was once so beautiful is dead.

Your hands once touched this table and this silver,
And I have seen your fingers hold this glass.
These things do not remember you, beloved,
And yet your touch upon them will not pass.

For it was in my heart that you moved among them,
And blessed them with your hands and with your eyes;
And in my heart they will remember always,
– They knew you once, O beautiful and wise.

"MUSIC TO HEAR, WHY HEAR'ST THOU MUSIC SADLY?"

Music to hear, why hear'st thou music sadly?
Sweets with sweets war not, joy delights in joy:
Why lov'st thou that which thou receiv'st not gladly,
Or else receiv'st with pleasure thine annoy?
If the true concord of well-tuned sounds,
By unions married, do offend thine ear,
They do but sweetly chide thee, who confounds
In singleness the parts that thou should'st bear:
Mark how one string, sweet husband to another,
Strikes each in each by mutual ordering,
Resembling sire, and child, and happy mother
Who, all in one, one pleasing note do sing:
    Whose speechless song, being many, seeming one,
    Sings this to thee: "Thou single wilt prove none".

SONG AND MUSIC

O leave your hand where it lies cool
Upon the eyes whose lids are hot:
Its rosy shade is bountiful
Of silence, and assuages thought.
O lay your lips against your hand
And let me feel your breath through it,
While through the sense your song shall fit
The soul to understand.

The music lives upon my brain
Between your hands within mine eyes;
It stirs your lifted throat like pain,
An aching pulse of melodies.
Lean nearer, let the music pause:
The soul may better understand
Your music, shadowed in your hand
Now while the song withdraws.

CELIA SINGING

You that think Love can convey
   No other way
But through the eyes, into the heart,
   His fatal dart,
Close up those casements, and but hear
   This siren sing;
   And on the wing
Of her sweet voice, it shall appear
That Love can enter at the ear.

Then unveil your eyes; behold
   The curious mould
Where that voice dwells, and as we know,
   When the cocks crow,
And Sol is mounted on his way,
   We freely may
   Gaze on the day;
So may you, when the music's done,
Awake, and see the rising sun.

From THE TAMING OF THE SHREW

"Why, then thou canst not break her to the lute?"
"Why no, for she hath broke the lute to me.
I did but tell her she mistook her frets,
And bow'd her hand to teach her fingering;
When, with a most impatient, devilish spirit,
'Frets call you these?' quoth she; 'I'll fume with them:'
And with that word she struck me on the head,
And through the instrument my pate made way;
And there I stood amazèd for a while,
As on a pillory, looking through the lute,
While she did call me rascal fiddler,
And twangling Jack, with twenty such vile terms,
As had she studied to misuse me so."

From THE HOUSE OF DUST: A SYMPHONY

The half-shut doors through which we heard that music
Are softly closed. Horns mutter down to silence.
The stars whirl out, the night grows deep.
Darkness settles upon us. A vague refrain
Drowsily teases at the drowsy brain.
In numberless rooms we stretch ourselves and sleep.

Where have we been? What savage chaos of music
Whirls in our dreams? – We suddenly rise in darkness,
Open our eyes, cry out, and sleep once more.
We dream we are numberless sea-waves languidly
        foaming
A warm white moonlit shore;

Or clouds blown windily over a sky at midnight,
Or chords of music scattered in hurrying darkness,
Or a singing sound of rain . . .
We open our eyes and stare at the coiling darkness,
And enter our dreams again.

THE FIDDLER

The fiddler knows what's brewing
   To the lilt of his lyric wiles:
The fiddler knows what rueing
   Will come of this night's smiles!

He sees couples join them for dancing,
   And afterwards joining for life,
He sees them pay high for their prancing
   By a welter of wedded strife.

He twangs: "Music hails from the devil,
   Though vaunted to come from heaven,
For it makes people do at a revel
   What multiplies sins by seven.

"There's many a heart now mangled,
   And waiting its time to go,
Whose tendrils were first entangled
   By my sweet viol and bow!"

GRATIANA DANCING AND SINGING

See! with what constant motion,
Even and glorious as the sun,
   Gratiana steers that noble frame,
Soft as her breast, sweet as her voice
That gave each winding law and poise,
   And swifter than the wings of Fame.

She beat the happy pavement
By such a star made firmament
   Which now no more the roof envies;
But swells up high, with Atlas even,
Bearing the brighter, nobler heaven,
   And, in her, all the deities.

Each step trod out a lover's thought
And the ambitious hopes he brought,
   Chained to her brave feet with such arts,
Such sweet command and gentle awe,
As, when she ceased, we sighing saw
   The floor lay paved with broken hearts.

So did she move; so did she sing,
Like the harmonious spheres that bring
   Unto their rounds their music's aid;
Which she performed such a way
As all the enamoured world will say,
   "The Graces danced, and Apollo played."

From VERSES

O fair! O sweet! when I do look on thee,
In whom all joys so well agree,
Just accord all music makes;
In thee just accord excelleth,
Where each part in such peace dwelleth,
One of other beauty takes.
Since then truth to all minds telleth,
That in thee lives harmony,
Heart and soul do sing in me.

MUSIC

I have been urged by earnest violins
And drunk their mellow sorrows to the slake
Of all my sorrows and my thirsting sins.
My heart has beaten for a brave drum's sake.

Huge chords have wrought me mighty: I have hurled
Thuds of God's thunder. And with old winds pondered
Over the curse of this chaotic world,
With low lost winds that maundered as they wandered.

I have been gay with trivial fifes that laugh;
And songs more sweet than possible things are sweet;
And gongs, and oboes. Yet I guessed not half
Life's sympathy till I had made hearts beat,
And touched Love's body into trembling cries,
And blown my love's lips into laughs and sighs.

TO HIS FRIEND MASTER R. L.,
IN PRAISE OF MUSIC AND POETRY

If music and sweet poetry agree,
As they must needs, the sister and the brother,
Then must the love be great 'twixt thee and me,
Because thou lov'st the one, and I the other.
Dowland to thee is dear, whose heavenly touch
Upon the lute doth ravish human sense;
Spenser, to me, whose deep conceit is such
As, passing all conceit, needs no defence.
Thou lov'st to hear the sweet melodious sound
That Phoebus' lute, the queen of music, makes;
And I in deep delight am chiefly drowned
Whenas himself to singing he betakes:
     One god is god of both, as poets feign;
     One knight loves both, and both in thee remain.

THE FAIR SINGER

To make a final conquest of all me,
    Love did compose so sweet an enemy,
In whom both beauties to my death agree,
    Joining themselves in fatal harmony:
That while she with her eyes my heart doth bind,
She with her voice might captivate my mind.

I could have fled from one but singly fair;
    My disentangled soul itself might save,
Breaking the curled trammels of her hair:
    But how should I avoid to be her slave,
Whose subtle art invisibly can wreathe
My fetters of the very air I breathe?

It had been easy fighting in some plain
    Where victory might hang in equal choice;
But all resistance against her is vain,
    Who has the advantage both of eyes and voice:
And all my forces needs must be undone,
She having gained both the wind and sun.

"HOW OFT WHEN THOU, MY MUSIC, MUSIC PLAY'ST"

How oft when thou, my music, music play'st
Upon that blessed wood whose motion sounds
With thy sweet fingers when thou gently sway'st
The wiry concord that mine ear confounds,
Do I envy those jacks that nimble leap
To kiss the tender inward of thy hand,
Whilst my poor lips, which should that harvest reap,
At the wood's boldness by thee blushing stand.
To be so tickled they would change their state
And situation with those dancing chips
O'er whom thy fingers walk with gentle gait,
Making dead wood more blest than living lips:
    Since saucy jacks so happy are in this,
      Give them thy fingers, me thy lips to kiss.

From CHILDE HAROLD'S PILGRIMAGE

Music arose with its voluptuous swell,
   Soft eyes look'd love to eyes which spake again,
     And all went merry as a marriage bell.

POP, ROCK

When I hear music, I fear no danger,
I am invulnerable, I see no foe . . .

HENRY DAVID THOREAU

HEAT

Here in the electric dusk your naked lover
tips the glass high and the ice cubes fall against
    her teeth.
It's beautiful Susan, her hair sticky with gin,
Our Lady of Wet Glass-Rings on the Album Cover,
streaming with hatred in the heat
as the record falls and the snake-band chords begin
to break like terrible news from the Rolling Stones,
and such a last light – full of spheres and zones.
August,
        you're just an erotic hallucination,
just so much feverishly produced kazoo music,
are you serious? – this large oven impersonating night,
this exhaustion mutilated to resemble passion,
the bogus moon of tenderness and magic
you hold out to each prisoner like a cup of light?

FIRST PARTY AT KEN KESEY'S
WITH HELL'S ANGELS

Cool black night thru the redwoods
cars parked outside in shade
behind the gate, stars dim above
the ravine, a fire burning by the side
porch and a few tired souls hunched over
in black leather jackets. In the huge
wooden house, a yellow chandelier
at 3 a.m. the blast of loudspeakers
hi-fi Rolling Stones Ray Charles Beatles
Jumping Joe Jackson and twenty youths
dancing to the vibration thru the floor,
a little weed in the bathroom, girls in scarlet
tights, one muscular smooth skinned man
sweating dancing for hours, beer cans
bent littering the yard, a hanged man
sculpture dangling from a high creek branch,
children sleeping softly in their bedroom bunks.
And 4 police cars parked outside the painted
gate, red lights revolving in the leaves.

PAINKILLERS

The King of rock 'n roll
grown pudgy, almost matronly,
Fatty in gold lamé,
mad King encircled
by a court of guards, suffering
delusions about assassination,
obsessed by guns, fearing
rivalry and revolt

popping his skin
with massive hits of painkiller

dying at 42.

What was the pain?
Pain had been the colours
of the bad boy with the sneer.

The story of pain, of separation,
was the divine comedy
he had translated
from black into white.

For white children too
the act of naming the pain
unsheathed
a keen joy at the heart of it.

Here they are still!
the disobedient
who keep a culture alive
by subverting it, turning
for example a subway
into a garden of graffiti.

But the puffy King
lived on, his painkillers
neutralizing, neutralizing,
until he became
ludicrous in performance.

The enthroned cannot revolt.
What was the pain
he needed to kill
if not the ultimate pain

of feeling no pain?

WAITING ON ELVIS, 1956

This place up in Charlotte called Chuck's where I
used to waitress and who came in one night
but Elvis and some of his friends before his concert
at the Arena, I was twenty-six married but still
waiting tables and we got to joking around like you
do, and he was fingering the lace edge of my slip
where it showed below my hemline and I hadn't even
seen it and I slapped at him a little saying, You
sure are the one aren't you feeling my face burn but
he was the kind of boy even meanness turned sweet in
his mouth.

Smiled at me and said, Yeah honey I guess I sure am.

THE SUPREMES

We were born to be gray. We went to school,
Sat in rows, ate white bread,
Looked at the floor a lot. In the back
Of our small heads

A long scream. We did what we could,
And all we could do was
Turn on each other. How the fat kids suffered!
Not even being jolly could save them.

And then there were the anal retentives,
The terrified brown-noses, the desperately
Athletic or popular. This, of course,
Was training. At home

Our parents shook their heads and waited.
We learned of the industrial revolution,
The sectioning of the clock into pie slices.
We drank cokes and twiddled our thumbs. In the
Back of our minds

A long scream. We snapped butts in the showers,
Froze out shy girls on the dance floor,
Pin-pointed flaws like radar.
Slowly we understood: this was to be the world.

We were born insurance salesmen and secretaries,
Housewives and short order cooks,
Stock room boys and repairmen,
And it wouldn't be a bad life, they promised,
In a tone of voice that would force some of us
To reach in self-defense for wigs,
Lipstick,

Sequins.

WOODY GUTHRIE VISITED BY
BOB DYLAN: BROOKLYN STATE
HOSPITAL, NEW YORK, 1961

He has lain here for a terrible, motionless
Decade, and talks through a system of winks
And facial twitches. The nurse props a cigarette
Between his lips, wipes his forehead. She thinks
He wants to send the kid away, but decides
To let him in – he's waited hours.
Guitar case, jean jacket. A corduroy cap slides
Down his forehead. Doesn't talk. He can't be more
Than twenty. He straps on the harmonica holder,
Tunes up, and begins his "Song to Woody,"
Trying to sound three times his age, sandpaper
Dustbowl growl, the song interminable, inept.
        Should he
Sing another? The eyes roll their half-hearted yes.
The nurse grits her teeth, stubs out the cigarette.

MR COGITO AND POP

1

During a pop concert
Mr Cogito mulls over
the aesthetics of noise

an idea in itself
quite appealing

being a god means
to hurl thunderbolts

or less theologically
to swallow the elements' tongue

to substitute an earthquake
for Homer
a stone avalanche
for Horace

to drag from guts
what's in the guts
terror and hunger

to lay bare the paths
of intestines
to lay bare the paths

of the breath
to lay bare the paths
of desire

to play mad love songs
on a red throat

2
the trouble is
that a cry eludes form
is poorer than a voice
which rises
and falls

a cry touches silence
but by way of hoarseness
not by way of the desire
to describe silence

its darkness blazes
with inarticulacy

it rejected the grace of humor
because it knows no half-tones

it is like a knife blade
driven into a mystery

it does not wrap itself
around the mystery
never finds its shapes

expresses emotional truths
from a wildlife reservation

it seeks the paradise lost
in a new jungle of order

prays for a violent death
and this will be granted

ZBIGNIEW HERBERT
TRANS. ALISSA VALLES

THE DEATH OF JANIS JOPLIN

October 4, 1970
Oh, Lord, won't you buy me
a Mercedes-Benz!

Because she was a white girl
    born black-and-blue,
because she was outsized victim
    of her own insides,
because she was voted
    "Ugliest Man on Campus,"
because she looked for something
    and found nothing –
    she became famous.

"Tell me that you love me!"
    she screamed at audiences.
They told. Fat Janis wouldn't
    believe. Twenty-seven,
a star since twenty-four,
    she tried to suck, lick,
smoke, shoot, drip, drop,
    drink the world.
    Nothing worked.

Bought a house, a place
    to go home to.
Bought a dog, something to give
    love to. Nothing worked.
Jimi Hendrix died, Janis cried:
    "Goddamn. He beat me
to it!" Not by much. Three weeks
    later she joined him.
    Part of something at last.

From SLEEVE NOTES

TALKING HEADS: *True Stories*

You can take the man out of Armagh but, you may ask
      yourself,
can you take the Armagh out of the man in the big
      Armani suit?

U2: *The Joshua Tree*

When I went to hear them in Giants Stadium
a year or two ago, the whiff
of kef
brought back the night we drove all night from Palm

Springs to Blythe. No Irish lad and his lass
were so happy as we who roared
and soared
through yucca-scented air. Dawn brought a sense of loss,

faint at first, that would deepen and expand
as our own golden chariot
was showered
with Zippo spears from the upper tiers of the stands.

NIRVANA: *Bleach*

I went there, too, with Mona, or Monica.
Another shot of Absolut.

"The Wild Rover" or some folk anthem
on the jukebox. Some dour

bartender. I, too, have been held fast
by those snares and nets

off the Zinc Coast, the coast of Zanzibar,
                              lost

                    able
                      addiction

               "chin-chins"
                              loos,

"And it's no,
nay, never, no nay never no more..."

JAZZ, BLUES

If ya ain't got it in ya, ya can't blow it out.
LOUIS ARMSTRONG

STRONG, OFF ROUTE 209

Armstrong
is blowing the roof off
over the coffee-stop's
back-of-the-counter
radio.

She puts down her coffee
and rides with him;
the old woman wings with him
out, into her upper airs.

When he starts to sing
she shuts her eyes
and mouths the words
right on time
delicious

Louis Armstrong, summa
cum laude, young Lester
Young's young University.

MOOD INDIGO

it hasnt always been this way
ellington was not a street
robeson no mere memory
du bois walked up my father's stairs
hummed some tune over me
sleeping in the company of men
who changed the world

it wasnt always like this
why ray barretto used to be a side-man
& dizzy's hair was not always gray
i remember   i was there
i listened in the company of men
politics as necessary as collards
music even in our dreams

our house was filled with all kinda folks
our windows were not cement or steel
our doors opened like our daddy's arms
held us safe & loved
children growing in the company of men
old southern men & young slick ones
sonny til was not a boy
the clovers no rag-tag orphans
our crooners/ we belonged to a whole world

nkrumah was no foreigner
virgil aikens was not the only fighter

it hasnt always been this way
ellington was not a street

ELEVEN
From *Velvet Bebop Kente Cloth*

There ain't/No word
I ain't/Heard.
ain't/No word
Bird/Ain't heard.

Language is an/Inventor's
privilege.

I/Blow psalms.
I/Blow sinners'deeds.
I/Blow prayer before death.
I/Blow curses.
I/Blow laughter.
I/Blow vocabulary of my axe.

You can't/Hold
folks/Down who Be-Bop
but you/Kin hold
them/Up.

Every Be-Bopper/Renew
his/Subscriptions
to/Genius when he riff some
thing/New on his axe.

TRANE

Propped against the crowded bar
he pours into the curved and silver horn
his old unhappy longing for a home

the dancers twist and turn
he leans and wishes he could burn
his memories to ashes like some old notorious emperor

of rome. but no stars blazed across the sky when he
     was born
no wise men found his hovel; this crowded bar
where dancers twist and turn,

holds all the fame and recognition he will ever earn
on earth or heaven. he leans against the bar
and pours his old unhappy longing in the saxophone

FOR MILES

Your sound is faultless
        pure & round
                holy
        almost profound

Your sound is your sound
        true & from within
        a confession
        soulful & lovely

Poet whose sound is played
        lost or recorded
        but heard
        can you recall that 54 night at the Open Door
        when you & bird
        wailed five in the morning some wondrous
        yet unimaginable score?

CANARY
For Michael S. Harper

Billie Holiday's burned voice
had as many shadows as lights,
a mournful candelabra against a sleek piano,
the gardenia her signature under that ruined face.

(Now you're cooking, drummer to bass,
magic spoon, magic needle.
Take all day if you have to
with your mirror and your bracelet of song.)

Fact is, the invention of women under siege
has been to sharpen love in the service of myth.

If you can't be free, be a mystery.

THE WEARY BLUES

Droning a drowsy syncopated tune,
Rocking back and forth to a mellow croon,
    I heard a Negro play.
Down on Lenox Avenue the other night
By the pale dull pallor of an old gas light
    He did a lazy sway....
    He did a lazy sway....
To the tune o' those Weary Blues.
With his ebony hands on each ivory key
He made that poor piano moan with melody.
    O Blues!
Swaying to and fro on his rickety stool
He played that sad raggy tune like a musical fool.
    Sweet Blues!
Coming from a black man's soul.
    O Blues!
In a deep song voice with a melancholy tone
I heard that Negro sing, that old piano moan –
    "Ain't got nobody in all this world,
    Ain't got nobody but maself.
    I's gwine to quit ma frownin'
    And put ma troubles on the shelf."
Thump, thump, thump, went his foot on the floor.
He played a few chords then he sang some more –
    "I got the Weary Blues

And I can't be satisfied.
Got the Weary Blues
And can't be satisfied –
I ain't happy no mo'
And I wish that I had died."
And far into the night he crooned that tune.
The stars went out and so did the moon.
The singer stopped playing and went to bed
While the Weary Blues echoed through his head.
He slept like a rock or a man that's dead.

WOMAN, I GOT THE BLUES

I'm sporting a floppy existential sky-blue hat
when we meet in the Museum of Modern Art.

Later, we hold each other
with a gentleness that would break open
ripe fruit. Then we slow-drag
to Little Willie John, we bebop
to Bird LPs, bloodfunk, lungs paraphrased
till we break each other's fall.
For us there's no reason the scorpion
has to become our faith healer.

Sweet Mercy, I worship
the curvature of your ass.
I build an altar in my head.
I kiss your breasts & forget my name.

Woman, I got the blues.
Our shadows on floral wallpaper
struggle with cold-blooded mythologies.
But there's a stillness in us
like the tip of a magenta mountain.
Half-naked on the living-room floor;
the moon falling through the window
on you like a rapist.

Your breath's a dewy flower stalk
leaning into sweaty air.

HOMAGE TO THE EMPRESS OF
THE BLUES

Because there was a man somewhere in a candystripe
    silk shirt,
gracile and dangerous as a jaguar and because a
    woman moaned
for him in sixty-watt gloom and mourned him
    Faithless Love
Twotiming Love Oh Love Oh Careless Aggravating
    Love,

    She came out on the stage in yards of pearls,
        emerging like
    a favorite scenic view, flashed her golden smile
        and sang.

Because gray laths began somewhere to show from
    underneath
torn hurdygurdy lithographs of dollfaced heaven;
and because there were those who feared alarming
    fists of snow
on the door and those who feared the riot-squad
    of statistics,

    She came out on the stage in ostrich feathers,
        beaded satin,
    and shone that smile on us and sang.

BED MUSIC

Our love was new,
But your bedsprings were old.
In the flat below,
They stopped eating
With forks in the air.

They made the old sourpuss
Climb the stairs
And squint through the keyhole,
While we went right ahead
Making the springs toot,

Playing "Low Down on the Bayou,"
Playing "Big Leg Mama,"
Playing "Shake It Baby"
And "Carolina Shout."

That was the limit!
They called the fire brigade.
They called the Law.
They could've brought some hooch,
We told the cops.

COMPOSERS

We were standing alone at the window when it started
to rain and Schumann quietly.

FRANZ WRIGHT

THE COMPOSER

All the others translate: the painter sketches
A visible world to love or reject;
Rummaging into his living, the poet fetches
The images out that hurt and connect.

From Life to Art by painstaking adaption,
Relying on us to cover the rift;
Only your notes are pure contraption,
Only your song is an absolute gift.

Pour out your presence, O delight, cascading
The falls of the knee and the weirs of the spine,
Our climate of silence and doubt invading;

You alone, alone, O imaginary song,
Are unable to say an existence is wrong,
And pour out your forgiveness like a wine.

MUSIC

BEETHOVEN

Music often takes me like a sea
    and I set out
under mist or a transparent sky
    for my pale star;

I run before the wind as if I had
    laid on full sail,
climbing the mountainous backs of the waves,
    plummeting down

in darkness, eardrums throbbing as I feel
    the coming wreck;
fair winds or foul – a raging storm

    on the great deep
my cradle, and dead calm the looking-glass
    of my despair!

MOZART, 1935

Poet, be seated at the piano.
Play the present, its hoo-hoo-hoo,
Its shoo-shoo-shoo, its ric-a-nic,
Its envious cachinnation.

If they throw stones upon the roof
While you practice arpeggios,
It is because they carry down the stairs
A body in rags.
Be seated at the piano.

That lucid souvenir of the past,
The divertimento;
That airy dream of the future,
The unclouded concerto...
The snow is falling.
Strike the piercing chord.

Be thou the voice,
Not you. Be thou, be thou
The voice of angry fear,
The voice of this besieging pain.

Be thou that wintry sound
As of the great wind howling,

By which sorrow is released,
Dismissed, absolved
In a starry placating.

We may return to Mozart.
He was young, and we, we are old.
The snow is falling
And the streets are full of cries.
Be seated, thou.

BACH CONCERTO

I never slept late in the morning,
the early trams would wake me,
and often my own verses.
They pulled me out of bed by my hair,
dragged me to my table,
and as soon as I'd rubbed my eyes
they made me write.

Bound by sweet saliva
to the lips of a unique moment,
I gave no thought
to the salvation of my miserable soul,
and instead of eternal bliss
I longed for a quick instant
of fleeting pleasure.

In vain did the bells try to lift me up:
I clung to the ground with tooth and nail.
It was full of fragrance
and exciting mysteries.
And when I gazed at the sky at night
I did not seek the heavens.
I was more afraid of the black holes
somewhere on the edge of the universe,
they are more terrible still
than hell itself.

But I caught the sound of a harpsichord.
It was a concerto
for oboe, harpsichord and strings
by Johann Sebastian Bach.
From where it came I do not know.
But clearly not from earth.

Although I had not drunk any wine
I swayed a little
and had to steady myself with
my own shadow.

THE SCARLATTI SUN

The mute seamstress on her knees
sticks a pin in the hem
and weeps for the cloth;

the dead stop their dying,
their heads warming like stones
in the Scarlatti sun;

the grave postman,
his worn leather bag strapped to his back,
feels his mind go, windswept.

An old woman at her window,
her old cat on the sill, sips thick coffee
from a saucer, and in the shuttered convent,

the novitiate, taken up,
rushes across the just-washed floor,
daring the ground to break a bone.

ROBERT SCHUMANN

Hardly a day passes I don't think of him
in the asylum: younger

than I am now, trudging the long road down
through madness toward death.

Everywhere in this world his music
explodes out of itself, as he

could not. And now I understand
something so frightening, and wonderful –

how the mind clings to the road it knows, rushing
through crossroads, sticking

like lint to the familiar. So!
Hardly a day passes I don't

think of him: nineteen, say, and it is
spring in Germany

and he has just met a girl named Clara.
He turns the corner,

he scrapes the dirt from his soles,
he runs up the dark staircase, humming.

ALLEGRO

After a black day, I play Haydn,
and feel a little warmth in my hands.

The keys are ready. Kind hammers fall.
The sound is spirited, green, and full of silence.

The sound says that freedom exists
and someone pays no tax to Caesar.

I shove my hands in my haydnpockets
and act like a man who is calm about it all.

I raise my haydnflag. The signal is:
"We do not surrender. But want peace."

The music is a house of glass standing on a slope;
rocks are flying, rocks are rolling.

The rocks roll straight through the house
but every pane of glass is still whole.

From THE DUNCIAD

"Oh cara, cara! silence all that train:
Joy to great Chaos! let division reign!
Chromatic tortures soon shall drive them hence,
Break all their nerves, and fritter all their sense:
One trill shall harmonise joy, grief, and rage,
Wake the dull Church, and lull the ranting stage.
To the same notes thy sons shall hum or snore,
And all thy yawning daughters cry 'encore.'
Another Phoebus – thy own Phoebus – reigns,
Joys in my jigs and dances in my chains.
But soon, ah, soon, rebellion will commence,
If music meanly borrows aid from sense:
Strong in new arms, lo, giant Handel stands,
Like bold Briareus, with a hundred hands:
To stir, to rouse, to shake the soul he comes,
And Jove's own thunders follow Mars's drums . . ."

HENRY PURCELL

*The poet wishes well to the divine genius of Purcell and
praises him that, whereas other musicians have given utter-
ance to the moods of man's mind, he has, beyond that, uttered
in notes the very make and species of man as created both in
him and in all men generally.*

Have fair fallen, O fair, fair have fallen, so dear
To me, so arch-especial a spirit as heaves in Henry
      Purcell,
An age is now since passed, since parted; with the
      reversal
Of the outward sentence low lays him, listed to a
      heresy, here.

Not mood in him nor meaning, proud fire or sacred fear,
Or love or pity or all that sweet notes not his might
      nursle:
It is the forgèd feature finds me; it is the rehearsal
Of own, of abrúpt sélf there so thrusts on, so throngs
      the ear.

Let him oh! with his air of angels then lift me, lay me!
      only I'll
Have an eye to the sakes of him, quaint moonmarks,
      to his pelted plumage under
Wings: so some great stormfowl, whenever he has
      walked his while

The thunder-purple seabeach plumèd purple-of-thunder,
If a wuthering of his palmy snow-pinions scatter a
    colossal smile
Off him, but meaning motion fans fresh our wits
    with wonder.

MUSIC
For D.D.S.*

A flame burns within her, miraculously,
While you look, her edges crystallize.
She alone will draw near and speak to me
When others are afraid to meet my eyes.
She was with me even in my grave
When the last of my friends turned away,
And she sang like the first storm heaven gave,
Or as if flowers were having their say.

*Dmitri D. Shostakovitch, 1906–75, Russian composer.

AN ARTIST IN THE NORTH

I, Edvard Grieg, moved free among men.
I joked a lot, read the papers, often on tour.
I conducted the orchestra.
The auditorium and its lights shuddered with each
    triumph like a train ferry pushing in to dock.

I have holed myself up here to butt heads with silence.
My work hut is small.
The grand piano fits as rubbing-tight in here as a
    swallow under a roof shingle.

The steep and lovely mountain slopes are silent most
    of the time.
There is no path
but there is a wicket that sometimes opens,
and a peculiar light leaks in directly from the trolls.

Simplify!

And hammer blows in the mountain came
came
came
came one spring night into our room
disguised as heartbeats.

The year before I die I shall send out four hymns
        to track down God.
But it begins here.
A song about that which is near.

That which is near.

Battlegrounds within us
where we Bones of the Dead
fight to come alive.

TOMAS TRANSTRÖMER
TRANS. MAY SWENSON

SEVENTEEN

The adolescent Franz Schubert,
seventeen, composes music
to the wails of Faust's Gretchen, a girl his own age.
Meine Ruh' ist hin, mein Herz ist schwer.
Immediately that noted talent scout, Death,
fawning all over him, signs him up.
Sends invitations, one after another.
One. After. Another. Schubert asks
for indulgence, he doesn't want to arrive
empty-handed. But how ungracious to refuse.
Fourteen years later he gives
his first concert on the other side.
Why does charity kill, why does being strong blind?
Meine Ruh' ist hin, mein Herz ist schwer.

126   ADAM ZAGAJEWSKI
      TRANS. RENATA GORCZYNSKI, BENJAMIN IVRY
      AND C. K. WILLIAMS

ON RACHMANINOFF'S BIRTHDAY

Blue windows, blue rooftops
and the blue light of the rain,
there contiguous phrases of Rachmaninoff
pouring into my enormous ears
and the tears falling into my blindness

for without him I do not play,
especially in the afternoon
on the day of his birthday. Good
fortune, you would have been
my teacher and I your only pupil

and I would always play again.
Secrets of Liszt and Scriabin
whispered to me over the keyboard
on unsunny afternoons! and growing
still in my stormy heart.

Only my eyes would be blue as I played
and you rapped my knuckles,
        dearest father of all the Russias,
        placing my fingers
tenderly upon your cold, tired eyes.

FRANK O'HARA   127

From CHOPIN

It was low and long,
Ivory white, with doors and windows blotting blue
    upon it.
Wind choked in pomegranate-trees,
Rain rattled on lead roofs,
And stuttered along twisted conduit-pipes.
An eagle screamed out of the heavy sky,
And some one in the house screamed
"Ah, I knew that you were dead!"

So that was it:
Funeral chants,
And the icy cowls of buried monks;
Organs on iron midnights,
And long wax winding-sheets
Guttered from altar candles.
First this,
Then spitting blood.
Music quenched in blood,
Flights of arpeggios confused by blood,
Flute-showers of notes stung and arrested on a
    sharp chord,
Tangled in a web of blood.
"I cannot send you the manuscripts, as they are not
    yet finished.

I have been ill as a dog.
My illness has had a pernicious effect on the Preludes
Which you will receive God knows when."

From TO RICHARD WAGNER

"Hark! Gay fanfares from halls of old Romance
    Strike through the clouds of clamor: who be these
That, paired in rich processional, advance
    From darkness o'er the murk mad factories
Into yon flaming road, and sink, strange Ministrants!
    Sheer down to earth, with many minstrelsies
And motions fine, and mix about the scene
    And fill the Time with forms of ancient mien?

"Bright ladies and brave knights of Fatherland;
    Sad mariners, no harbor e'er may hold,
A swan soft floating tow'rds a magic strand;
    Dim ghosts, of earth, air, water, fire, steel, gold,
Wind, grief, and love; a lewd and lurking band
    Of Powers – dark Conspiracy, Cunning cold,
Gray Sorcery; magic cloaks and rings and rods;
    Valkyries, heroes, Rhinemaids, giants, gods!
                    *   *   *
"O Wagner, westward bring thy heavenly art,
    No trifler thou: Siegfried and Wotan be
Names for big ballads of the modern heart.
    Thine ears hear deeper than thine eyes can see.
Voice of the monstrous mill, the shouting mart,
    Not less of airy cloud and wave and tree,
Thou, thou, if even to thyself unknown,
    Hast power to say the Time in terms of tone."

From CHOPIN

A voice was needed, sweet and true and fine
As the sad spirit of the evening breeze,
Throbbing with human passion, yet devine
As the wild bird's untutored melodies.
A voice for him 'neath twilight heavens dim,
Who mourneth for his dead, while round him fall
The wan and noiseless leaves. A voice for him
Who sees the first green sprout, who hears the call
Of the first robin on the first spring day.
A voice for all whom Fate hath set apart,
Who, still misprized, must perish by the way,
Longing with love, for that they lack the art
Of their own soul's expression. For all these
Sing the unspoken hope, the vague, sad reveries.

POULENC

My first day in Paris I walked
            from Saint Germain to the Pont Mirabeau
in soft amber light and leaves
            and love was running out

city of light and hearts
            city of dusk and dismay
the Seine believed it to be true
            that I was unloved and alone

how lonely is that bridge
            without your song
the Avenue Mozart, the rue Pergolèse
            the tobaccos and the nuns

all Paris is alone for this
            brief leafless moment
and snow falls down upon
            the streets of our peculiar hearts

THE OPUS

Music excavates Heaven.
CHARLES BAUDELAIRE

A PRAYER AGAINST STRAUSS'
"SALOMÉ," 1900

Sir Edward Elgar, so he told Frederick Delius,
was urged by New York's religious to pray
for the failure of Richard Strauss' new opera, "Salomé":

O Saint Cecilia, won't you intercede today
and stop this opera before it can blight us?
May its orchestra squint with conjunctivitis,
split lips afflict entire wind sections,
brass players be seized with random infections,
dropsies bloat the fiddlers' fingers,
and blessed Cecilia, as for the singers,
May the eponymous lead soprano,
who spouts so shamelessly Strauss' guano,
swell to bursting and grow a beard,
so the heathen present at the premiered
work mistake her for Wagner's late held-
entenor, Ludwig Schnorr von Carolsfeld.
Swathe the brazen hussy in reinforced concrete
and hang her over the Danube River by her feet
to waltzes by the *veritable* Strauss, Johann,
not this godless, uncivilized barbarian.

SONNET ON HEARING THE DIES IRAE SUNG IN THE SISTINE CHAPEL

Nay, Lord, not thus! white lilies in the spring,
Sad olive-groves, or silver-breasted dove,
Teach me more clearly of Thy life and love
Than terrors of red flame and thundering.
The hillside vines dear memories of Thee bring:
A bird at evening flying to its nest
Tells me of One who had no place of rest:
I think it is of Thee the sparrows sing.
Come rather on some autumn afternoon,
When red and brown are burnished on the leaves,
And the fields echo to the gleaner's song,
Come when the splendid fulness of the moon
Looks down upon the rows of golden sheaves,
And reap Thy harvest: we have waited long.

LISTENING TO DVOŘÁK'S
SERENADE IN E

Everything has ripened,
the oranges glisten
in their sharp worlds,
the apples have broken
their juice
in my mouth,
I am alone at the edge
of all the gold seasons,
a tide of clouds
bearing me home
like a migratory bird.

And this bright music
shaping dancers
on a bitter dust of roads,
divining rods
that point
to a further distance:
stone, water, stone.

Dowser, find my deep stream.
Builder, make my house
to last in the ochre heart
of the falling sun,
in this shining harvest.

COLETTE INEZ

THE NINTH SYMPHONY OF BEETHOVEN
UNDERSTOOD AT LAST AS A SEXUAL
MESSAGE

A man in terror of impotence
or infertility, not knowing the difference
a man trying to tell something
howling from the climacteric
music of the entirely
isolated soul
yelling at Joy from the tunnel of the ego
music without the ghost
of another person in it, music
trying to tell something the man
does not want out, would keep if he could
gagged and bound and flogged with chords of Joy
where everything is silence and the
beating of a bloody fist upon
a splintered table

From STRAVINSKY'S THREE PIECES
"GROTESQUES," FOR STRING QUARTET

FIRST MOVEMENT
Thin-voiced, nasal pipes
Drawing sound out and out
Until it is a screeching thread,
Sharp and cutting, sharp and cutting,
It hurts.
Whee-e-e!
Bump! Bump! Tong-ti-bump!
There are drums here,
Banging,
And wooden shoes beating the round, grey stones
Of the market-place.
Whee-e-e!
Sabots slapping the worn, old stones,
And a shaking and cracking of dancing bones;
Clumsy and hard they are,
And uneven,
Losing half a beat
Because the stones are slippery.
Bump-e-ty-tong! Whee-e-! Tong!
The thin Spring leaves
Shake to the banging of shoes.
Shoes beat, slap,
Shuffle, rap,

And the nasal pipes squeal with their pigs' voices,
Little pigs' voices
Weaving among the dancers,
A fine white thread
Linking up the dancers,
Bang! Bump! Tong!
Petticoats,
Stockings,
Sabots,
Delirium flapping its thigh-bones;
Red, blue, yellow,
Drunkenness steaming in colours;
Red, yellow, blue,
Colours and flesh weaving together,
In and out, with the dance,
Coarse stuffs and hot flesh weaving together.
Pigs' cries white and tenuous,
White and painful,
White and –
Bump!
Tong!

LINES: TO A MOVEMENT IN MOZART'S E-FLAT SYMPHONY

Show me again the time
When in the Junetide's prime
We flew by meads and mountains northerly! –
Yea, to such freshness, fairness, fulness, fineness,
        freeness,
    Love lures life on.

Show me again the day
When from the sandy bay
We looked together upon the pestered sea! –
Yea, to such surging, swaying, sighing, swelling,
        shrinking,
    Love lures life on.

Show me again the hour
When by the pinnacled tower
We eyed each other and feared futurity! –
Yea, to such bodings, broodings, beatings, blanchings,
        blessings,
    Love lures life on.

Show me again just this:
The moment of that kiss
Away from the prancing folk, by the strawberry-tree! –
Yea, to such rashness, ratheness, rareness, ripeness,
        richness,
    Love lures life on.

From THE MAJOR-GENERAL'S SONG
The Pirates of Penzance

I am the very model of a modern Major-General,
I've information vegetable, animal, and mineral,
I know the kings of England, and I quote the fights
        historical
From Marathon to Waterloo, in order categorical;
I'm very well acquainted, too, with matters
        mathematical;
I understand equations, both the simple and
        quadratical,
About binomial theorem I'm teeming with a
        lot o' news,
With many cheerful facts about the square of the
        hypotenuse.

I'm very good at integral and differential calculus;
I know the scientific names of beings animalculous:
In short, in matters vegetable, animal, and mineral,
I am the very model of a modern Major-General.

I know our mythic history, King Arthur's and
        Sir Caradoc's;
I answer hard acrostics, I've a pretty taste for paradox,
I quote in elegiacs all the crimes of Heliogabalus,
In conics I can floor peculiarities parabolous;

I can tell undoubted Raphaels from Gerard Dows
      and Zoffanies,
I know the croaking chorus from *The Frogs*
      of Aristophanes!
Then I can hum a fugue of which I've heard the
      music's din afore,
And whistle all the airs from that infernal nonsense
      Pinafore.

BRAHMS' CLARINET QUINTET
IN B MINOR, OP. 115

That we shall not forget to honour
brown, its reedy clarities.

And, though the earth is dying
and the names of its diseases
spread from the fencelines, Latinate:
a bright field
ribboned with swath.

That the mind's light could be filtered
as: a porch, late afternoon,
a trellised rose,
                    which is to say
a truth in nostalgia:
if we steel ourselves against regret
we will not grow more graceful,
but less.

That a letter might honestly
begin, *Dear beloved.*

A MINUET OF MOZART'S

Across the dimly lighted room
The violin drew wefts of sound,
Airily they wove and wound
And glimmered gold against the gloom.

I watched the music turn to light,
But at the pausing of the bow,
The web was broken and the glow
Was drowned within the wave of night.

THE VICTOR DOG
for Elizabeth Bishop

Bix to Buxtehude to Boulez,
The little white dog on the Victor label
Listens long and hard as he is able.
It's all in a day's work, whatever plays.

From judgment, it would seem, he has refrained.
He even listens earnestly to Bloch,
Then builds a church upon our acid rock.
He's man's – no – he's the Leiermann's best friend,

Or would be if hearing and listening were the same.
Does he hear? I fancy he rather smells
Those lemon-gold arpeggios in Ravel's
"Les jets d'eau du palais de ceux qui s'aiment."

He ponders the Schumann Concerto's tall willow hit
By lightning, and stays put. When he surmises
Through one of Bach's eternal boxwood mazes
The oboe pungent as a bitch in heat,

Or when the calypso decants its raw bay rum
Or the moon in *Wozzeck* reddens ripe for murder,
He doesn't sneeze or howl; just listens harder.
Adamant needles bear down on him from

Whirling of outer space, too black, too near –
But he was taught as a puppy not to flinch,
Much less to imitate his bête noire Blanche
Who barked, fat foolish creature, at King Lear.

Still others fought in the road's filth over Jezebel,
Slavered on hearths of horned and pelted barons.
His forebears lacked, to say the least, forbearance.
Can nature change in him? Nothing's impossible.

The last chord fades. The night is cold and fine.
His master's voice rasps through the grooves'
        bare groves.
Obediently, in silence like the grave's
He sleeps there on the still-warm gramophone

Only to dream he is at the première of a Handel
Opera long thought lost – *Il Cane Minore*.
Its allegorical subject is his story!
A little dog revolving round a spindle

Gives rise to harmonies beyond belief,
A cast of stars . . . Is there in Victor's heart
No honey for the vanquished? Art is art.
The life it asks of us is a dog's life.

JAMES MERRILL   147

From THE SYMPHONY

A velvet flute-note fell down pleasantly
Upon the bosom of that harmony,
And sailed and sailed incessantly,
As if a petal from a wild-rose blown
Had fluttered down upon that pool of tone
And boatwise dropped o' the convex side
And floated down the glassy tide
And clarified and glorified
The solemn spaces where the shadows bide.
From the warm concave of that fluted note
Somewhat, half song, half odor, forth did float,
As if a rose might somehow be a throat.

BACH FUGUE

Frees the horses from their mechanical bolts,
Keeps the fire from spreading to the sleepers' floor.
The miming dancers in the wings (*swell to great*)
Begin their sly whisperings, their tired arms
Around each other's waists. The old woman spoons
    yellow cake
Into her (*celestial tremulous*) mouth. Capable of putting
Poor Gloucester's eyes, glistening, back. Catches the
    jumpers
With invisible nets from their sad, night bridges;
Finds all those who have been lost to you. The great
Chords, once struck, can never decay.

THE HARLOT'S HOUSE

We caught the tread of dancing feet,
We loitered down the moonlit street,
And stopped beneath the harlot's house.

Inside, above the din and fray,
We heard the loud musicians play
The "Treues Liebes Herz" of Strauss.

Like strange mechanical grotesques,
Making fantastic arabesques,
The shadows raced across the blind.

We watched the ghostly dancers spin
To sound of horn and violin,
Like black leaves wheeling in the wind.

Like wire-pulled automatons,
Slim silhouetted skeletons
Went sidling through the slow quadrille.

They took each other by the hand,
And danced a stately saraband;
Their laughter echoed thin and shrill.

Sometimes a clockwork puppet pressed
A phantom lover to her breast,
Sometimes they seemed to try to sing.

Sometimes a horrible marionette
Came out, and smoked its cigarette
Upon the steps like a live thing.

Then, turning to my love, I said,
"The dead are dancing with the dead,
The dust is whirling with the dust."

But she – she heard the violin,
And left my side, and entered in:
Love passed into the house of lust.

Then suddenly the tune went false,
The dancers wearied of the waltz,
The shadows ceased to wheel and whirl.

And down the long and silent street,
The dawn, with silver-sandalled feet,
Crept like a frightened girl.

INSTRUMENTS

And yet this were surely a gain, to heal men's
Wounds by music's spell.

EURIPIDES

From THE MYSTIC TRUMPETER

O trumpeter, methinks I am myself the instrument
  thou playest,
Thou melt'st my heart, my brain – thou movest,
  drawest, changest them at will;
And now thy sullen notes send darkness through me,
Thou takest away all cheering light, all hope,
I see the enslaved, the overthrown, the hurt, the
  opprest of the whole earth,
I feel the measureless shame and humiliation of my
  race, it becomes all mine,
Mine too the revenges of humanity, the wrongs of
  ages, baffled feuds and hatreds,
Utter defeat upon me weighs – all lost – the foe
  victorious,
(Yet 'mid the ruins Pride colossal stands unshaken
  to the last,
Endurance, resolution to the last.)

Now trumpeter for thy close,
Vouchsafe a higher strain than any yet,
Sing to my soul, renew its languishing faith and hope,
Rouse up my slow belief; give me some vision of the
  future,
Give me for once its prophecy and joy.

O glad, exulting, culminating song!
A vigor more than earth's is in thy notes,
Marches of victory – man disenthral'd – the conqueror
    at last,
Hymns to the universal God from universal man –
    all joy!
A reborn race appears – a perfect world, all joy!
Women and men in wisdom innocence and health –
    all joy!
Riotous laughing bacchanals fill'd with joy!
War, sorrow, suffering gone – the rank earth purged –
    nothing but joy left!
The ocean fill'd with joy – the atmosphere all joy!
Joy! joy! in freedom, worship, love! joy in the ecstasy
    of life!
Enough to merely be! enough to breathe!
Joy! joy! all over joy!

WHEN THE VIOLIN

When
The violin
Can forgive the past

It starts singing.

When the violin can stop worrying
About the future

You will become
Such a drunk laughing nuisance

That God
Will then lean down
And start combing you into
His
Hair.

When the violin can forgive
Every wound caused by
Others

The heart starts
Singing.

HAFIZ
TRANS. DANIEL LADINSKY

CELLO

Those who don't like it say it's
just a mutant violin
that's been kicked out of the chorus.
Not so.
The cello has many secrets,
but it never sobs,
just sings in its low voice.
Not everything turns into song
though. Sometimes you catch
a murmur or a whisper:
I'm lonely,
I can't sleep.

PIANO

Softly, in the dusk, a woman is singing to me;
Taking me back down the vista of years, till I see
A child sitting under the piano, in the boom of the
     tingling strings
And pressing the small, poised feet of a mother who
     smiles as she sings.

In spite of myself, the insidious mastery of song
Betrays me back, till the heart of me weeps to belong
To the old Sunday evenings at home, with winter
     outside
And hymns in the cosy parlour, the tinkling piano
     our guide.

So now it is vain for the singer to burst into clamour
With the great black piano appassionato. The glamour
Of childish days is upon me, my manhood is cast
Down in the flood of remembrance, I weep like a child
     for the past.

THE CLARINET

All the klezmer bands used it,
When they eased themselves down from dark,
Down down down down.

Prospero broke his black staff,
And vainglorious light beamed out:
The fairy-light, slave-light, chalumeau blue

Music foot-flatted in the New Englander barn,
Moon-thin and rumbled bass yeses and linnets,
And sounded-out vanilla sugar;

Quavers of coloraturas
Made tintinnabulation and allargando,
As the valve trombone and guitar

Hush hush in the background
And got cool-quiet and waked the blues,
Listen listen and the light come through.

THE GUITAR

The weeping of the guitar
begins.
The goblets of dawn
are smashed.
The weeping of the guitar
begins.
Useless
to silence it.
Impossible
to silence it.
It weeps monotonously
as water weeps
as the wind weeps
over snowfields.
Impossible
to silence it.
It weeps for distant
things.
Hot southern sands
yearning for white camellias.
Weeps arrow without target
evening without morning
and the first dead bird
on the branch.
Oh, guitar!
Heart mortally wounded
by five swords.

FEDERICO GARCÍA LORCA
TRANS. COLA FRANZEN

161

From THE BELLS

Hear the sledges with the bells –
Silver bells!
What a world of merriment their melody foretells!
How they tinkle, tinkle, tinkle,
In the icy air of night!
While the stars that oversprinkle
All the heavens seem to twinkle
With a crystalline delight;
Keeping time, time, time,
In a sort of Runic rhyme,
To the tintinnabulation that so musically wells
From the bells, bells, bells, bells,
Bells, bells, bells –
From the jingling and the tinkling of the bells.

"HARP OF WILD AND DREAM LIKE STRAIN"

Harp of wild and dream like strain
When I touch thy strings
Why dost thou repeat again
Long forgotten things?

Harp in other earlier days
I could sing to thee
And not one of all my lays
Vexed my memory

But now if I awake a note
That gave me joy before
Sounds of sorrow from thee float
Changing evermore

Yet still steeped in memory's dyes
They come sailing on
Darkening all my summer skies
Shutting out my sun

From COME YE SONS OF ART
Ode by Henry Purcell for the birthday of Queen Mary II

Come, ye Sons of Art, come away,
Tune all your voices and instruments play,
To celebrate this triumphant day.

Sound the trumpet, till around
You make the listening shores rebound.
On the sprightly hautboy play,
All the instruments of joy
That skilful numbers can employ
To celebrate the glories of this day.

Come, ye Sons of Art, come away,
Tune all your voices and instruments play,
To celebrate this triumphant day.

Strike the viol, touch the lute,
Wake the harp, inspire the flute,
Sing your patroness's praise
In cheerful and harmonious lays.

From THE AEOLIAN HARP
Composed at Clevedon, Somersetshire

My pensive Sara! thy soft cheek reclined
Thus on mine arm, most soothing sweet it is
To sit beside our cot, our cot o'ergrown
With white-flowered jasmin, and the broad-leaved
    myrtle,
(Meet emblems they of Innocence and Love!)
And watch the clouds, that late were rich with light,
Slow saddening round, and mark the star of eve
Serenely brilliant (such should wisdom be)
Shine opposite! How exquisite the scents
Snatched from yon bean-field! and the world so hushed!
The stilly murmur of the distant sea
Tells us of silence.

            And that simplest lute,
Placed length-ways in the clasping casement, hark!
How by the desultory breeze caressed,
Like some coy maid half yielding to her lover,
It pours such sweet upbraiding, as must needs
Tempt to repeat the wrong! And now, its strings
Boldlier swept, the long sequacious notes
Over delicious surges sink and rise,
Such a soft floating witchery of sound
As twilight Elfins make, when they at eve

Voyage on gentle gales from Fairy-Land,
Where Melodies round honey-dropping flowers,
Footless and wild, like birds of Paradise,
Nor pause, nor perch, hovering on untamed wing!
O the one life within us and abroad,
Which meets all motion and becomes its soul,
A light in sound, a sound-like power in light,
Rhythm in all thought, and joyance every where –
Methinks, it should have been impossible
Not to love all things in a world so filled;
Where the breeze warbles, and the mute still air
Is Music slumbering on her instrument.

"BLAME NOT MY LUTE"

Blame not my lute, for he must sound
Of this or that as liketh me;
For lack of wit the lute is bound
To give such tunes as pleaseth me:
Though my songs be somewhat strange,
And speaks such words as touch thy change,
        Blame not my lute.

My lute, alas, doth not offend,
Though that perforce he must agree
To sound such tunes as I intend
To sing to them that heareth me:
Then though my songs be somewhat plain
And toucheth some that use to feign,
        Blame not my lute.

My lute and strings may not deny,
But, as I strike, they must obey:
Break not them then so wrongfully,
But wreak thyself some wiser way,
And, though the songs which I indite
Do quit thy change with rightful spite,
        Blame not my lute.

Spite asketh spite, and changing change,
And falsed faith must needs be known;
The fault so great, the case so strange,
Of right it must abroad be blown:
Then since that by thine own desert
My songs do tell how true thou art,
      Blame not my lute.

Blame but thyself that hast misdone
And well deserved to have blame:
Change thou thy ways so evil begun,
And then my lute shall sound that same.
But if till then my fingers play
By thy desert their wonted way,
      Blame not my lute.

Farewell, unknown, for though thou break
My strings in spite with great disdain,
Yet have I found out for thy sake
Strings for to string my lute again.
And if perchance this foolish rhyme
Do make thee blush at any time,
      Blame not my lute.

THE FLUTE

This childhood recollection moves me even now:
The day our village flutist, laughing, showed me how
To hold the flute to my unpractised mouth. And he,
Then, close against his heart, set me upon his knee;
Declared I was a master, rivaling his skill,
And shaped my childish lips, though all uncertain still.
He taught me how to breathe a long, pure note; and then,
With my young fingers in his knowing hands, again
And yet again he guided them until they could,
Of their own will, draw music from a tube of wood.

ANDRÉ CHÉNIER   169
TRANS. LLOYD ALEXANDER

From FRUIT-GATHERING

Listen, my heart, in his flute is the music of the smell of wild flowers, of the glistening leaves and gleaming water, of shadows resonant with bee's wings.

  The flute steals his smile from my friend's lips and spreads it over my life.

From THE CREMONA VIOLIN

Above all things, above Charlotta his wife,
Herr Altgelt loved his violin, a fine
Cremona pattern, Stradivari's life
Was flowering out of early discipline
When this was fashioned. Of soft-cutting pine
The belly was. The back of broadly curled
Maple, the head made thick and sharply whirled.

The slanting, youthful sound-holes through
The belly of fine, vigorous pine
Mellowed each note and blew
It out again with a woody flavour
Tanged and fragrant as fir-trees are
When breezes in their needles jar.

The varnish was an orange-brown
Lustered like glass that's long laid down
Under a crumbling villa stone.
Purfled stoutly, with mitres which point
Straight up the corners. Each curve and joint
Clear, and bold, and thin.
Such was Herr Theodore's violin.

"THE TONGUES OF VIOLINS!"

The tongues of violins!
(I think, O tongues, ye tell this heart, that cannot
    tell itself;
This brooding, yearning heart, that cannot tell itself.)

From THE PRINCESS

The splendour falls on castle walls
    And snowy summits old in story:
The long light shakes across the lakes,
    And the wild cataract leaps in glory,
Blow, bugle, blow, set the wild echoes flying,
Blow, bugle; answer, echoes, dying, dying, dying.

O hark, O hear! how thin and clear,
    And thinner, clearer, farther going!
O sweet and far from cliff and scar
    The horns of Elfland faintly blowing!
Blow, let us hear the purple glens replying:
Blow, bugle; answer, echoes, dying, dying, dying.

O love, they die in yon rich sky,
    They faint on hill or field or river:
Our echoes roll from soul to soul,
    And grow for ever and for ever.
Blow, bugle, blow, set the wild echoes flying,
And answer, echoes, answer, dying, dying, dying.

ALFRED, LORD TENNYSON   173

TRUMPETS

Trumpets blare under trimmed willows where tanned
Children play and leaves drift. Graveyard-shudders.
Scarlet flags plunge through the grief of maples,
Riders in ryefields, and empty mills.

Or shepherds sing at night, and deer step
Into the circle of their fire, the forest's ancient sorrow.
Dancers rise from a black wall –
Scarlet flags, laughter, madness, trumpets.

VIOLIN

A violin is naked. It has skinny little arms. Clumsily it tries to cover itself with them. It sobs for shame and cold. That's why. Not, as the music reviewers say, to make it more beautiful. That's simply not true.

HARP

The water is shallow. In the water the light is golden and flat. In silver reeds, the wind's fingers clasp the one salvaged column.

A black girl clasps a harp. Her great Egyptian eye swims among strings like a mournful fish. A long way behind it, little fingers.

HARPSICHORD

In fact it is a cupboard made of walnut in a black frame. You might think that it is used to keep yellowing letters, Gypsy coins, and ribbons – whereas there's nothing but a cuckoo entangled in a thicket of silver leaves.

From JUBILATE AGNO

For the spiritual music is as follows:

For there is the thunder-stop, which is the voice of
     God direct.

For the rest of the stops are by their rhymes.

For the trumpet rhymes are bound, soar, more and
     the like.

For the shawm rhymes are lawn, fawn, moon, boom and
     the like.

For the harp rhymes are sing, ring, string and the like.

For the cymbal rhymes are bell, well, toll, soul and
     the like.

For the flute rhymes are tooth, youth, suit, mute and
     the like.

For the dulcimer rhymes are grace, place, beat, heat and
     the like.

For the clarinet rhymes are clean, seen and the like.

For the bassoon rhymes are pass, class, and the like.
     God be gracious to Baumgarden.

For the dulcimer are rather van, fan and the like and
     grace, place etc. are of the bassoon.

For beat, heat, weep, peep, etc. are of the pipe.

For every word has its marrow in the English tongue
     for order and for delight.

For the dissyllables such as able, table, etc. are the
     fiddle rhymes.

For all dissyllables and some trisyllables are
     fiddle rhymes.

BEAT! BEAT! DRUMS!

Beat! beat! drums! – blow! bugles! blow!
Through the windows – through doors – burst like a
        ruthless force,
Into the solemn church, and scatter the congregation,
Into the school where the scholar is studying;
Leave not the bridegroom quiet – no happiness must
        he have now with his bride,
Nor the peaceful farmer any peace, ploughing his field
        or gathering his grain,
So fierce you whirr and pound you drums – so shrill
        you bugles blow.

Beat! beat! drums! – blow! bugles! blow!
Over the traffic of cities – over the rumble of wheels
        in the streets;
Are beds prepared for sleepers at night in the houses?
        no sleepers must sleep in those beds,
No bargainers' bargains by day – no brokers or
        speculators – would they continue?
Would the talkers be talking? would the singer
        attempt to sing?
Would the lawyer rise in the court to state his case
        before the judge?
Then rattle quicker, heavier drums – you bugles
        wilder blow.

Beat! beat! drums! – blow! bugles! blow!
Make no parley – stop for no expostulation,
Mind not the timid – mind not the weeper or prayer,
Mind not the old man beseeching the young man,
Let not the child's voice be heard, nor the mother's
     entreaties,
Make even the trestles to shake the dead where they
     lie awaiting the hearses,
So strong you thump O terrible drums – so loud you
     bugles blow.

From IL PENSEROSO

There let the pealing organ blow,
   To the full voiced quire below,
      In service high, and anthems clear,
         As may with sweetness, through mine ear,
            Dissolve me into ecstasies,
               And bring all heaven before mine eyes.

"I HEARD YOU SOLEMN-SWEET PIPES OF THE ORGAN"

I heard you solemn-sweet pipes of the organ as last
    Sunday morn I pass'd the church,
Winds of autumn, as I walk'd the woods at dusk I heard
    your long-stretch'd sighs up above so mournful,
I heard the perfect Italian tenor singing at the opera,
    I heard the soprano in the midst of the quartet
    singing;
Heart of my love! you too I heard murmuring low
    through one of the wrists around my head,
Heard the pulse of you when all was still ringing little
    bells last night under my ear.

TO THE SORROW STRING

You invisible one
resounding on your own
whatever the others
happen to be playing
source of a note
not there in the score
under whatever key
unphrased continuo
gut stretched between
the beginning and the end
what would the music
be without you
since even through
the chorus of pure joy
the tears hear you
and nothing can restrain them

From HAMLET

Why, look you now, how unworthy a thing you make of
me! You would play upon me; you would seem to know
my stops; you would pluck out the heart of my
mystery; you would sound me from my lowest note to
the top of my compass: and there is much music,
excellent voice, in this little organ; yet cannot
you make it speak. 'Sblood, do you think I am
easier to be played on than a pipe? Call me what
instrument you will, though you can fret me, yet you
cannot play upon me.

VOICE

Do you know that our soul is composed of harmony.

LEONARDO DA VINCI

LAURA

Rose-cheeked Laura, come;
Sing thou smoothly with thy beauty's
Silent music, either other
        Sweetly gracing.

Lovely forms do flow
From concent divinely framed;
Heaven is music, and thy beauty's
        Birth is heavenly.

These dull notes we sing
Discords need for helps to grace them;
Only beauty purely loving
        Knows no discord;

But still moves delight,
Like clear springs renewed by flowing,
Ever perfect, ever in them-
        Selves eternal.

SINGER

Far from the world, poetic magic intoxicates him;
   for him beautiful verses are the whole world.
Fantasy has built for her songster
   a strong house of the spirit that destiny cannot shake.

You may say, "Life is cold and futile. It is folly
   to think that life consists of the pleasant
sounds of a flute, and nothing else." Or, "Hard
    insensibility
   lashes the one who was never wracked by the pain

of the struggle of life." But your judgment
   is delusion and injustice. His Nature is divine.
Judge not in your logical, blind sickness.

The walls of his house are of magic emerald –
   and voices within them whisper, "Friend, be quiet;
meditate and sing. Be of good heart, mystic apostle!"

COLORATURA

Poised beneath a twig-wigged tree,
she spills her sparkling vocal powder:
slippery sound slivers, silvery
like spider's spittle, only louder.

Oh yes, she Cares (with a high C)
for Fellow Humans (you and me);
for us she'll twitter nothing bitter;
she'll knit her fitter, sweeter glitter;
her vocal cords mince words for us
and crumble croutons, with crisp crunch
(lunch for her little lambs to munch)
into a cream-filled demitasse.

But hark! It's dark! Oh doom too soon!
She's threatened by the black bassoon!
It's hoarse and coarse, it's grim and gruff,
it calls her dainty voice's bluff –
Basso Profundo, end this terror,
do-re-mi mene tekel et cetera!

You want to silence her, abduct her
to our chilly life behind the scenes?
To our Siberian steppes of stopped-up sinuses,
frogs in all throats, eternal hems and haws,
where we, poor souls, gape soundlessly
like fish? And this is what you wish?

Oh nay! Oh nay! Though doom be nigh,
she'll keep her chin and pitch up high!
Her fate is hanging by a hair
of voice so thin it sounds like *air*,
but that's enough for her to take
a breath and soar, without a break,
chandelierward; and while she's there,
her vox humana crystal-clears
the whole world up. And we're all ears.

From THE RING CYCLE

Brünnhilde confronts Siegfried. That is to say,
Two singers have been patiently rehearsed
So that their tones and attitudes convey
Outrage and injured innocence. But first
Two youngsters became singers, strove to master
Every nuance of innocence and outrage
Even in the bosom of their stolid
Middleclass families who made it possible
To study voice, and languages, take lessons
In how the woman loves, the hero dies . . .
Tonight again, each note a blade reforged,
The dire oath ready in their blood is sworn.
Two world-class egos, painted, overweight,
Who'll joke at supper side by side, now hate
So plausibly that one old stagehand cries.

ITALIAN MUSIC IN DAKOTA

[*"The Seventeenth – the finest Regimental Band
I ever heard."*]

Through the soft evening air enwinding all,
Rocks, woods, fort, cannon, pacing sentries,
    endless wilds,
In dulcet streams, in flutes' and cornets' notes,
Electric, pensive, turbulent, artificial,
(Yet strangely fitting even here, meanings
    unknown before,
Subtler than ever, more harmony, as if born here,
    related here,
Not to the city's fresco'd rooms, not to the audience
    of the opera house,
Sounds, echoes, wandering strains, as really here
    at home,
Sonnambula's innocent love, trios with *Norma's* anguish,
And thy ecstatic chorus *Poliuto*;)
Ray'd in the limpid yellow slanting sundown,
Music, Italian music in Dakota.

While Nature, sovereign of this gnarl'd realm,
Lurking in hidden barbaric grim recesses,
Acknowledging rapport however far remov'd,
(As some old root or soil of earth its last-born flower
    or fruit,)
Listens well pleas'd.

From AN OPERA HOUSE

Within the gold square of the proscenium arch,
A curtain of orange velvet hangs in stiff folds,
Its tassels jarring slightly when someone crosses the
    stage behind.
Gold carving edges the balconies,
Rims the boxes,
Runs up and down fluted pillars.
Little knife-stabs of gold
Shine out whenever a box door is opened.
Gold clusters
Flash in soft explosions
On the blue darkness,
Suck back to a point,
And disappear.
Hoops of gold
Circle necks, wrists, fingers,
Pierce ears,
Poise on heads
And fly up above them in coloured sparkles.
Gold!
Gold!
The opera house is a treasure-box of gold.
Gold in a broad smear across the orchestra pit:
Gold of horns, trumpets, tubas;
Gold – spun-gold, twittering-gold, snapping-gold

Of harps.
The conductor raises his baton,
The brass blares out
Crass, crude,
Parvenu, fat, powerful,
Golden.

From PROUD MUSIC OF THE STORM

All songs of current lands come sounding 'round me,
The German airs of friendship, wine and love,
Irish ballads, merry jigs and dances – English warbles,
Chansons of France, Scotch tunes – and o'er the rest,
Italia's peerless compositions.

Across the stage, with pallor on her face, yet lurid
        passion,
Stalks Norma, brandishing the dagger in her hand.

I see poor crazed Lucia's eyes' unnatural gleam;
Her hair down her back falls loose and dishevell'd.

I see where Ernani, walking the bridal garden,
Amid the scent of night-roses, radiant, holding his
        bride by the hand,
Hears the infernal call, the death-pledge of the horn.

To crossing swords, and gray hairs bared to heaven,
The clear, electric base and baritone of the world,
The trombone duo – Libertad forever!

                *   *   *

I hear the annual singing of the children in St Paul's
     Cathedral;
Or, under the high roof of some colossal hall, the
     symphonies, oratorios of Beethoven, Handel,
     or Haydn;
The Creation, in billows of godhood laves me.

Give me to hold all sounds, (I, madly struggling, cry,)
Fill me with all the voices of the universe,
Endow me with their throbbings – Nature's also,
The tempests, waters, winds – operas and chants –
     marches and dances,
Utter – pour in – for I would take them all.

UPON JULIA'S VOICE

So smooth, so sweet, so silvery is thy voice,
As, could they hear, the damned would make no noise,
But listen to thee, walking in thy chamber,
Melting melodious words to lutes of amber.

THE SOLITARY REAPER

Behold her, single in the field,
    Yon solitary Highland Lass!
Reaping and singing by herself;
    Stop here, or gently pass!
Alone she cuts and binds the grain,
And sings a melancholy strain;
O listen! for the Vale profound
Is overflowing with the sound.

No Nightingale did ever chaunt
    More welcome notes to weary bands
Of travellers in some shady haunt,
    Among Arabian sands:
A voice so thrilling ne'er was heard
In spring-time from the Cuckoo-bird,
Breaking the silence of the seas
Among the farthest Hebrides.

Will no one tell me what she sings? –
    Perhaps the plaintive numbers flow
For old, unhappy, far-off things,
    And battles long ago:
Or is it some more humble lay,
Familiar matter of today?
Some natural sorrow, loss, or pain,
That has been, and may be again?

Whate'er the theme, the Maiden sang
      As if her song could have no ending;
I saw her singing at her work,
      And o'er the sickle bending; –
I listen'd, motionless and still;
And, as I mounted up the hill,
The music in my heart I bore,
Long after it was heard no more.

"WHEN TO HER LUTE CORINNA SINGS"

When to her lute Corinna sings,
Her voice revives the leaden strings,
And doth in highest notes appear
As any challenged echo clear.
But when she doth of mourning speak,
E'en with her sighs the strings do break.

And as her lute doth live or die,
Led by her passion, so must I.
For when of pleasure she doth sing,
My thoughts enjoy a sudden spring;
But if she doth of sorrow speak,
E'en from my heart the strings do break.

HOW A LITTLE GIRL SANG

Ah, she was music in herself,
A symphony of joyousness.
She sang, she sang from finger tips,
From every tremble of her dress.
I saw sweet haunting harmony,
An ecstasy, an ecstasy,
In that strange curling of her lips,
That happy curling of her lips.
And quivering with melody
Those eyes I saw, that tossing head.

And so I saw what music was,
Tho' still accursed with ears of lead.

UPON A RARE VOICE

When I but hear her sing, I fare
Like one that, raised, holds his ear
To some bright star in the supremest round;
Through which, besides the light that's seen,
There may be heard, from heaven within,
The rest of anthems that the angels sound.

From DON JUAN

The devil hath not, in all his quiver's choice,
    An arrow for the heart like a sweet voice.

THE SINGER'S HOUSE

When they said *Carrickfergus* I could hear
the frosty echo of saltminers' picks.
I imagined it, chambered and glinting,
a township built of light.

What do we say any more
to conjure the salt of our earth?
So much comes and is gone
that should be crystal and kept,

and amicable weathers
that bring up the grain of things,
their tang of season and store,
are all the packing we'll get.

So I say to myself *Gweebarra*
and its music hits off the place
like water hitting off granite.
I see the glittering sound

framed in your window,
knives and forks set on oilcloth,
and the seals' heads, suddenly outlined,
scanning everything.

People here used to believe
that drowned souls lived in the seals.
At spring tides they might change shape.
They loved music and swam in for a singer

who might stand at the end of summer
in the mouth of a whitewashed turf-shed,
his shoulder to the jamb, his song
a rowboat far out in evening.

When I came here first you were always singing,
a hint of the clip of the pick
in your winnowing climb and attack.
Raise it again, man. We still believe what we hear.

ON A VOLUNTEER SINGER

Swans sing before they die – 'twere no bad thing
Did certain persons die before they sing.

LESSONS, PRACTICE

Who hears music, feels his solitude
Peopled at once.

ROBERT BROWNING

MUSICIAN

Where have these hands been,
By what delayed,
That so long stayed
Apart from the thin

Strings which they now grace
With their lonely skill
Music and their cool will
At last interlace.

Now with great ease, and slow,
The thumb, the finger, the strong
Delicate hand plucks the long
String it was born to know.

And, under the palm, the string
Sings as it wished to sing.

DEATH OF A PIANIST

While others waged war
or sued for peace, or lay
in narrow beds in hospitals
or camps, for days on end

he practiced Beethoven's sonatas,
and slim fingers, like a miser's,
touched great treasures
that weren't his.

ADAM ZAGAJEWSKI
    TRANS. CLARE CAVANAGH

THE SINGING LESSON

You must stand erect but at your ease, a posture
Demanding a compromise
Between your spine and your head, your best face
    forward,
Your willful hands
Not beckoning or clenching or sweeping upward
But drawn in close:
A man with his arms spread wide is asking for it,
A martyred beggar,
A flightless bird on the nest dreaming of flying.
For your full resonance
You must keep your inspiring and expiring moments
Divided but equal,
Not locked like antagonists from breast to throat,
Choking toward silence.

If you have learned, with labor and luck, the measures
You were meant to complete,
You may find yourself before an audience
Singing into the light,
Transforming the air you breathe – that malleable
    wreckage,
That graveyard of shouts,
That inexhaustible pool of chatter and whimpers –
Into deathless music.

But remember, with your mouth wide open, eyes shut,
Some men will wonder,
When they look at you without listening, whether
You're singing or dying.
Take care to be heard. But even singing alone,
Singing for nothing,
Singing to empty space in no one's honor,
Keep time: it will tell
When you must give the final end-stopped movement
Your tacit approval.

PIANO LESSONS

1

My teacher lies on the floor with a bad back
off to the side of the piano.
I sit up straight on the stool.
He begins by telling me that every key
is like a different room
and I am a blind man who must learn
to walk through all twelve of them
without hitting the furniture.
I feel myself reach for the first doorknob.

2

He tells me that every scale has a shape
and I have to learn how to hold
each one in my hands.
At home I practice with my eyes closed.
C is an open book.
D is a vase with two handles.
G flat is a black boot.
E has the legs of a bird.

3

He says the scale is the mother of the chords.
I can see her pacing the bedroom floor
waiting for her children to come home.

They are out at nightclubs shading and lighting
all the songs while couples dance slowly
or stare at one another across tables.
This is the way it must be. After all,
just the right chord can bring you to tears
but no one listens to the scales,
no one listens to their mother.

4
I am doing my scales,
the familiar anthems of childhood.
My fingers climb the ladder of notes
and come back down without turning around.
Anyone walking under this open window
would picture a girl of about ten
sitting at the keyboard with perfect posture,
not me slumped over in my bathrobe, disheveled,
like a white Horace Silver.

5
I am learning to play
"It Might As Well Be Spring"
but my left hand would rather be jingling
the change in the darkness of my pocket
or taking a nap on an armrest.
I have to drag him into the music
like a difficult and neglected child.

This is the revenge of the one who never gets
to hold the pen or wave good-bye,
and now, who never gets to play the melody.

6

Even when I am not playing, I think about the piano.
It is the largest, heaviest,
and most beautiful object in this house.
I pause in the doorway just to take it all in.
And late at night I picture it downstairs,
this hallucination standing on three legs,
this curious beast with its enormous moonlit smile.

VARIABLE

Vary, re-vary; tune and tune again
   (Anon to this string, and anon to that;
Bass, treble, tenor; swift, slow, sharp and flat)
Thy one same subject in a sundry strain,
To represent, by thy so diverse ditties,
   The dying world's so diverse alterations:
   Yet will the world have still more variations,
And, past thy verse, thy various subject yet is.

BALLATA
of True and False Spring

A little wild bird sometimes at my ear
Sings his own little verses very clear:
Others sing louder that I do not hear.

For singing loudly is not singing well;
But ever by the song that's soft and low
The master-singer's voice is plain to tell.
Few have it, and yet all are masters now,
And each of them can trill out what he calls
His ballads, canzonets, and madrigals.

The world with masters is so covered o'er
There is no room for pupils any more.

THE NOTES

I was not the right age to begin
to be taught to play the violin
Dr Perpetuo told my father
when I was four with these very hands
were we too young in his opinion
or were we already too old by then
I come now with no real preparation
to finger the extinct instruments
that I know only by reputation
after these years of trying to listen
to learn what I was listening for
what it is that I am trying to hear
it is something I had begun
giving ear to all unknown
before that day with its explanation
about the strings and how before you can
play the notes you have to make each one
I never even learned how to listen

TO A DAUGHTER AT FOURTEEN
FORSAKING THE VIOLIN

All year, Mozart went under
the sea of rock punk reggae
that crashed into your room every
night and wouldn't recede however
I sandbagged our shore
and swore to keep the house dry.
Your first violin, that halfsize
rented model, slipped out of tune
as you played Bach by ear
Suzuki method with forty other virtuosos
who couldn't tie their shoes.
Then such progress: your own
fiddle, the trellised notes you read,
recitals where I sat on hard chairs.

Your playing made me the kid.
If I had those fingers! ...
Five of yours grasped my pinky,
the world before you grew teeth.
O.K. They're your fingers.
To paint the nails of, put rings on,
hold cigarettes in, make obscene
gestures or farewells with.

MUSIC AT THE CLOSE

... you are the music
While the music lasts.

T. S. ELIOT

THE PLAYERS ASK FOR A BLESSING ON
THE PSALTERIES AND ON THEMSELVES

THREE VOICES [*together*]:
Hurry to bless the hands that play,
The mouths that speak, the notes and strings,
O masters of the glittering town!
O! lay the shrilly trumpet down,
Though drunken with the flags that sway
Over the ramparts and the towers,
And with the waving of your wings.

FIRST VOICE:
Maybe they linger by the way.
One gathers up his purple gown;
One leans and mutters by the wall –
He dreads the weight of mortal hours.

SECOND VOICE:
O no, O no! they hurry down
Like plovers that have heard the call.

THIRD VOICE:
O kinsmen of the Three in One,
O kinsmen, bless the hands that play.
The notes they waken shall live on
When all this heavy history's done;
Our hands, our hands must ebb away.

THREE VOICES [*together*]:
The proud and careless notes live on,
But bless our hands that ebb away.

From RICHARD II

The setting-sun, and music at the close,
As the last taste of sweets, is sweetest last,
Writ in remembrance more than things long past.

From HYMNE TO GOD MY GOD,
IN MY SICKNESSE

Since I am comming to that Holy roome,
   Where, with thy Quire of Saints for evermore,
I shall be made thy Musique; As I come
   I tune the Instrument here at the dore,
   And what I must doe then, thinke here before.

AN EPITAPH UPON THE CELEBRATED CLAUDY PHILIPS, MUSICIAN, WHO DIED VERY POOR

Philips, whose touch harmonious could remove
The pangs of guilty pow'r and hapless love,
Rest here, distress'd by poverty no more,
Here find that calm, thou gav'st so oft before.
Sleep, undisturb'd, within this peaceful shrine,
Till angels wake thee, with a note like thine.

(MUSIC)

Take me by the hand;
it's so easy for you, Angel,
for you are the road
even while being immobile.

You see, I'm scared no one
here will look for me again;
I couldn't make use of
whatever was given,

so they abandoned me.
At first the solitude
charmed me like a prelude,
but so much music wounded me.

From THE TEMPEST

Where should this music be? i' the air or the earth?
It sounds no more: and sure, it waits upon
Some god o' the island. Sitting on a bank,
Weeping again the king my father's wreck,
This music crept by me upon the waters,
Allaying both their fury and my passion
With its sweet air: thence I have follow'd it,
Or it hath drawn me rather. But 'tis gone.
No, it begins again.

IN A MUSEUM

Here's the mould of a musical bird long passed
        from light,
Which over the earth before man came was winging;
There's a contralto voice I heard last night,
That lodges in me still with its sweet singing.

Such a dream is Time that the coo of this ancient bird
Has perished not, but is blent, or will be blending
Mid visionless wilds of space with the voice that
        I heard,
In the full-fugued song of the universe unending.

THE PAVILION OF MUSIC

The musicians have gone.
The lilacs which they placed
   in the vases of jade
   bend toward the lutes
   and seem to listen still.

CHANG-WOU-KIEN
TRANS. ANON.

From THE SONNETS TO ORPHEUS

A tree ascended there. Oh pure transcendence!
Oh Orpheus sings! Oh tall tree in the ear!
And all things hushed. Yet even in that silence
a new beginning, beckoning, change appeared.

Creatures of stillness crowded from the bright
unbound forest, out of their lairs and nests;
and it was not from any dullness, not
from fear, that they were so quiet in themselves,

but from simply listening. Bellow, roar, shriek
seemed small inside their hearts. And where there
        had been
just a makeshift hut to receive the music,

a shelter nailed up out of their darkest longing,
with an entryway that shuddered in the wind –
you built a temple deep inside their hearing.

From ODE ON A GRECIAN URN

Heard melodies are sweet, but those unheard
   Are sweeter; therefore, ye soft pipes, play on;
      Not to the sensual ear, but, more endear'd,
         Pipe to the spirit ditties of no tone.

From CHANGED

I cannot sing the old songs now!
   It is not that I deem them low;
'Tis that I can't remember how
   They go.

From IDYLLS OF THE KING

It is the little rift within the lute
    That by and by will make the music mute,
        And ever widening slowly silence all.

From TO AUTUMN

Where are the songs of Spring? Ay, where are they?
    Think not of them, thou hast thy music too, –
While barred clouds bloom the soft-dying day,
    And touch the stubble-plains with rosy hue;
Then in a wailful choir the small gnats mourn
        Among the river sallows, borne aloft
            Or sinking as the light wind lives or dies;
And full-grown lambs loud bleat from hilly bourn;
        Hedge-crickets sing; and now with treble soft
        The red-breast whistles from a garden-croft;
            And gathering swallows twitter in the skies.

"LEAVES SCARCELY BREATHING"

Leaves scarcely breathing
in the black breeze;
the flickering swallow
draws circles in the dusk.

In my loving
dying heart
a twilight is coming,
a last ray, gently reproaching.

And over the evening forest
the bronze moon climbs to its place.
Why has the music stopped?
Why is there such silence?

OSIP MANDELSTAM   235
TRANS. CLARENCE BROWN AND W. S. MERWIN

"THE SUBLIME IS
A DEPARTURE"

The sublime is a departure.
Instead of following, something
in us starts going its own way
and getting used to heavens.

Isn't art's extreme encounter
the tenderest farewell?
And music: that last glance
that we ourselves throw back at us!

INDEX OF AUTHORS

245

ACKNOWLEDGMENTS

Thanks are due to the following copyright holders for permission to reprint:

CONRAD AIKEN: "Music I Heard" and excerpt from "The House of Dust, a Symphony" by Conrad Aiken, from *Collected Poems*, Copyright © 1915, 1920, 1943. Oxford University Press. Reprinted by permission of Brandt & Hochman Literary Agents, Inc. ANNA AKHMATOVA: "Music" from *Anna Akhmatova: Poems* by Anna Akhmatova, translated by Lyn Coffin. Copyright © 1983 by Lyn Coffin. Used by permission of W. W. Norton & Company, Inc. W. H. AUDEN: "The Composer", copyright © 1976 by Edward Mendelson, William Meredith and Monroe K. Spears, Executors of the Estate of W. H. Auden, from *Collected Poems* by W. H. Auden. Used by permission of Random House, Inc. "The Composer" from *Collected Poems* by W. H. Auden. Used by permission of Faber & Faber Limited. CHARLES BAUDELAIRE: "Music" from *Les Fleurs du mal* by Charles Baudelaire, translated from the French by Richard Howard. Reprinted by permission of David R. Godine, Publisher, Inc. Translation copyright © 1982 by Richard Howard. ELIZABETH BISHOP: "Sonnet" by Elizabeth Bishop, from *The Complete Poems*. Reprinted by permission of Farrar, Straus and Giroux, LLC. LOUISE BOGAN: "Musician" from *The Blue Estuaries* by Louise Bogan. Reprinted by permission of Farrar, Straus and Giroux, LLC. KAMAU BRATHWAITE: "Trane" by Kamau Brathwaite, from *Black + Blues*, copyright © 1976, 1994, 1995 by Kamau Brathwaite. Reprinted by permission of New Directions Publishing Corp. CONSTANTINE CAVAFY: "Singer" from *The Complete Poems of Cavafy*, translated by Rae Dalven, published by Chatto & Windus. Reprinted by permission of The Random House Group Limited. "Singer" from *The Complete Poems of Cavafy*, English translation copyright © 1961 and renewed 1989 by Rae Dalven, reprinted by permission of Houghton Mifflin Harcourt Publishing Company. CHANG-WOU-KIEN: "The Pavilion of Music" by Chang-Wou-Kien, found in *In Praise of Music* (Orion

254